little bento

Little Bento

32 IRRESISTIBLE BENTO BOX LUNCHES FOR KIDS

MICHELE OLIVIER

SONOMA
PRESS

For general information on our other products and services or to obtain technical support, please contact our Customer Care Department within the U.S. at (866) 744-2665, or outside the United States at (510) 253-0500.

Sonoma Press publishes its books in a variety of electronic and print formats. Some content that appears in print may not be available in electronic books, and vice versa.

TRADEMARKS: Sonoma Press and the Sonoma Press logo are trademarks or registered trademarks of Callisto Media Inc. and/or its affiliates, in the United States and other countries, and may not be used without written permission. All other trademarks are the property of their respective owners. Sonoma Press is not associated with any product or vendor mentioned in this book.

Photography © 2016 by Michele Olivier

Illustrations © Amy Sullivan

ISBN: Print 978-1-94345-128-9 | eBook 978-1-94345-129-6

To E&P, I'll eat you up I love you so

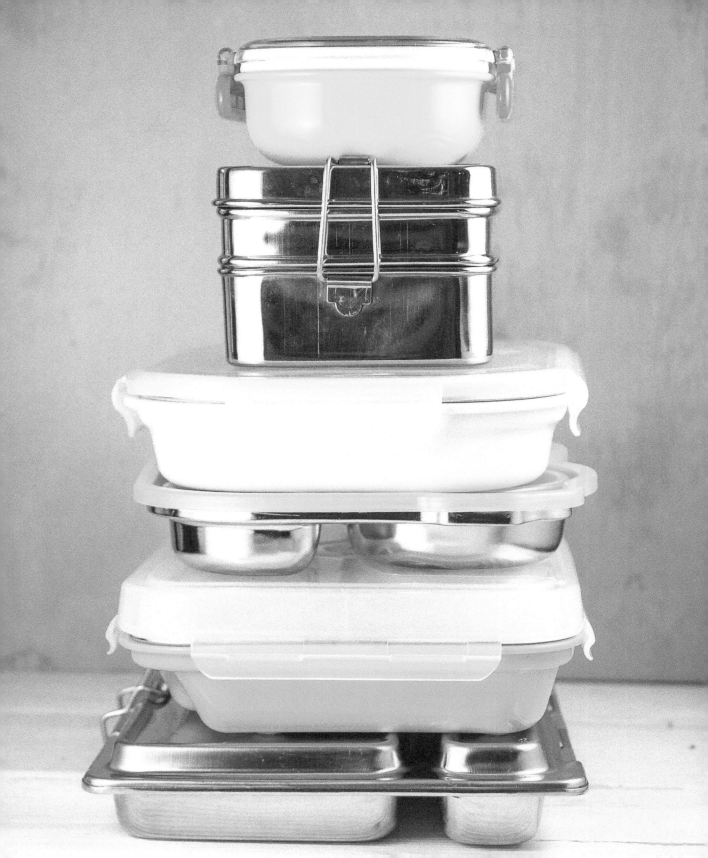

Contents

INTRODUCTION

When my first daughter, Ellie, was a baby, I went a little crazy making purées for her—and eating many of them myself. My commitment to preparing purées that were healthy, delicious, and adventurously seasoned has since expanded to include toddler and family meals as Ellie (now four) and her sister, Parker (now two), grow older.

To say that I love to make and feed my kids healthy food is an understatement. Now, as a parent, full-time food blogger, and cookbook author, it's my mission.

So, it comes as no surprise to anyone who knows me that when Ellie started preschool, I quickly became a little obsessed with sending her off each day with the healthiest, yummiest, and prettiest lunches—but only ones I could toss together in a short amount of time. Because even though I love making food, spending all day in the kitchen packing school lunches is not my thing.

Enter bento boxes. The organizer and planner in me was drawn to them. Okay, the shopper, too. The first thing I did was buy a couple of pretty bento boxes for Ellie's lunch storage. The next thing I did was buy some functional bento boxes that stored and actually held the food in place. Today, I have over 20 bento boxes and my husband jokes about having to build a shed

to warehouse them all. He might be on to something there.

I won't lie: The first week of packing bento box lunches was tough. It took me forever because I had no plan. Every morning I would stand in front of my pantry, drinking my second (or third) cup of coffee, waiting for some magical lunch idea to hit me. It never did. Ellie's lunches that first week of school were unbalanced and uninspired. If I wanted to send her to school with the best lunches, I had to go into planning mode—specifically, meal planning.

The key to packing amazing, efficient lunches comes down to three things:

1. PLAN YOUR FAMILY DINNERS AHEAD OF TIME. Planning dinners with leftovers that work for lunches is key to your sanity. This can be a big pot of chili you make on Sunday and then serve in a thermos on Tuesday. Or it can mean you use some leftover grilled chicken in a cheesy kale quesadilla later in the week.

2. BE REALISTIC. Life is busy, so having a couple of easy lunches to toss together in a pinch is pretty much essential. In trying out the recipes in this book, learn which you can make the fastest from staples you always have on hand.

3. FIND A TIME THAT WORKS FOR YOU. I cannot make lunches in the morning. It stresses me

out to add yet another task to our already busy morning routine. I find that making lunches is easier at night. My kitchen is already a mess and I can toss things into the bento boxes as I prep for dinner.

While it might seem as if you have to give this healthy lunch–packing thing a lot of fore-thought, I promise you that it will all become second nature. Well, maybe not second nature, but not extreme torture, which is how I think most of us feel about packing school lunches for 180 to 260 days a year.

And while this book focuses on school lunches for kids, the best part is that all of these recipes are meant for the entire family. So whatever I pack for Ellie's lunch also gets packed, in a smaller portion, for Parker's lunch, and in a big-ger portion, along with a salad, for my husband and myself. That's four healthy and delicious bento lunches packed at the same time. Can I get a high five?

The purpose of this book is not only to provide you with healthy, whole food recipes but also to give you pointers, meal-planning tips, and shortcuts for arranging those foods into bal-anced, irresistible bento lunches. While there are plenty of recipes in this book, that's not all it is. It's here to inspire your daily lunch making and to showcase a variety of foods that kids are likely to eat—that are also good for them. Some familiar, some new, all put together with other foods that make the whole box look too good not to eat. With dozens of beautiful bentos and kid-friendly recipes, I hope you will be able to use this book for years to come. Enjoy!

Bento 101

If you're paging through this book, you probably already know how popular bento boxes have become, and it's likely that more than half of the kids in your child's class are taking bento boxes to school. While there are tons of Pinterest boards and blog posts popping up with ideas on what to pack in them, it can still be a challenge deciding what the heck to choose. In this chapter I'm going to go over the basics of bento boxes, including which ones are my favorites, and some packing techniques and tips for parents with picky eaters. Then we'll get down to business and start making some of the 125+ recipes I have in here for you. Who's ready?

A MEAL, NOT A WORK OF ART

When I think of Japanese-style bento boxes for kids, foods cut into an array of cute characters and shapes immediately come to mind. And while I do have a degree in art, my ability to create an Olaf—you know, the beloved snowman of *Frozen* fame—out of cheese and rice is almost zilch. As cute (or *kawaii*, the Japanese word) as they are, this popular style of bento boxes also tends to lack the key nutritional elements and variety that I know are so important to offer in my kids' lunches. Here's my thinking:

KIDS WANT FOOD, NOT (JUST) FLUFFY ANIMALS. Above all, kids love their lunches bursting with the vibrant colors of whole foods—rich red strawberries, megawatt orange slices, bright yellow pepper sticks, intense green basil pesto, or dark shiny blackberries. Putting together a box full of rainbow colors will grab their attention and get them thinking about what to try first. Including small amounts of some of their favorite snacks and treats, like Sweet Cajun Party Mix (page 78) or Olive Oil + Walnut Brownies (page 118), will win their hearts—and tummies. I admit, cute shapes can be fun, but they're only new and unexpected the first few times you do them. For kids, predictable gets old fast.

HEALTHY NOT PROCESSED. By healthy, I mean a balanced, whole foods–based meal. I don't worry about including foods that are high in fat or carbohydrates—our kids are growing, after all. I make a point of packing lunches that include healthy fats, complex carbohydrates, a good amount of protein, and fresh produce. Snacks can be the trickiest part of a lunch. On some days, packing a processed snack option is the only way to get a snack in. I still do it in a pinch, though this book includes a bunch of healthy snack options. Do what you can and what time allows, no judgment here. Just keep in mind that the goal is to pack a lunch every day with balanced foods that will help your kids be naturally energetic, allow them to be alert and focused during class, and prevent them from an energy crash in the afternoon (which, as an added bonus, will hopefully curb after-school meltdowns, too).

NO WASTE. Packing lunches in bento boxes creates little to no waste and saves you from buying (and tossing) hundreds of plastic bags a year. Bento boxes are also, for the most part, pretty durable and can get tossed around from the day-to-day activities of your kids. Or is it just my kid who finds throwing her lunch bag into the air and letting it crash to the ground the most entertaining game?

A BEVY OF BENTO BOX OPTIONS

Finding the perfect bento box for your child is half the battle. I can't tell you how many hours I researched different boxes, box accessories, and packing methods. In the end, I just bought them all, which, I must admit, is not the most budget-friendly method.

There are any number of box options available. What I needed was a guide to help me figure out which bentos would work best for me. If only there had been a guide! Why wasn't there a guide? Fine, I finally told myself, I'll write my own guide. In the following sections, I give the details about important considerations with bento boxes. You'd be surprised at how much there is to think about, including shape, size, style, and material. I've also included what I like and don't like about them. You can find an even more comprehensive review of actual brands and their bento boxes on my blog.

Let's start with the basics. Here's a short list of what I think is important for you, as a parent, to consider when shopping for your child's first bento box.

Shapes

There are many different shapes of bento boxes, from oval, square, and rectangle to toddler-friendly designs like a school bus. As far as I'm concerned, slightly rounded corners are crucial—for both the box itself and the compartments inside. Rounded corners on the outside keeps kids from scratching themselves, and rounded corners inside make it easier for smaller kids—namely, my two-year-old—to scoop food out. What I don't like is that while some of the nontraditional shapes are fun for the kids, they are difficult to fit into most standard-size lunch bags. So, think twice about letting your kid pick out her new bento box.

Sizes and Styles

Where to begin? There are any number of bento sizes available, from small ones with just one or two compartments—perfect for snacks—to those with as many as five compartments, each of different sizes. Making a choice should come down to how many foods you plan to pack each day, and the amount of each. Some of my friends swear by a three-part lunch, day in and day out: main dish, fruit, wild card (vegetable, yogurt, crackers, and so on), while others always use a five-compartment bento. This book will showcase bentos ranging from one compartment to five. Look them over and see what appeals to you—both visually and in terms of what you can realistically prepare.

Personally, I like having options—recall the 20+ bento boxes I'm storing. If I had to narrow it down to only two bento boxes, though, I'd pick one with two or three compartments (snack or small lunch size) and one with five compartments (full meal size). Some days, I don't have it in me to make more than one meal, so I'll add a couple of easy things to the other compartments. Other days, I feel more creative and get excited about surprising my daughters with a treasure trove of food choices. (Keep in mind that boxes with lots of compartments tend to have lots of *small* compartments, so you're still not going to have to make a ton of food.)

There are some style variations, too, such as stacking bentos and those with snap-on lids (as opposed to affixed lids). The stacking boxes are clever, but they don't really work for my family. My preschooler simply will not unstack them, so some of what I prepare typically doesn't get eaten. Stacking bentos, however, might be ideal for an older child. The issue is similar with snap-on lids. They can be difficult for kids to remove, but if your younger children are in a daycare or preschool setting where teachers can help, no problem.

Portability

My biggest complaint with most bento boxes is that while the box itself might be leakproof, that's not necessarily the case for each individual compartment. This means that if there are any juices from your chopped fruit salad, they might spill over to your seed butter + jelly sandwich. Also, the food itself might transfer to other compartments when your kid travels to school, so what was an organized and cute bento box when it left the house is a messy pile of food when your child opens it. So, look for boxes that have individual leakproof compartments or, if you find a some-what impractical box that you love, know going into it you will have to buy separate containers to hold liquid items such as yogurt, applesauce, and pudding.

Material

Plastic or stainless steel? It's all about budget, preference, and your opinion on safe materials. Plastic bento boxes (both box and lid) should be free of BPA, phthalates, and lead. BPA and phthalates are chemicals used in many industrial plastics, including water bottles. If you send your kids to school with foods that do not need to be microwaved, plastic can be ideal, especially since it tends to be less expensive. Stainless-steel options should be made of the highest grade materials and be PVC- and lead-free. One of the risks of stainless steel is that it can dent. Personally, a little dent never bothered me (or prevented me from packing lunch), but it can be annoying

BENTO THEN AND NOW

The word "bento" is a Japanese term used to describe a meal in a box. Bentos have been a part of Japanese culture for more than 400 years. In the sixteenth century, a military commander fed his soldiers meals served in individual containers. It wasn't long before others, especially outdoor workers like farmers and fishermen, were using bentos while in the fields or on a boat. The meals were simple and built around rice—a staple of Japanese cuisine. Sometimes rice was mixed with millet or potatoes. Along with fruit, the food was packed into a simple container made of wood or leaves.

Fast-forward to today, and the bento box is as popular as ever in Japan—and skyrocketing in popularity elsewhere. Many Japanese schools require students to bring a bento every day. This has sparked the trend of chara-ben, or "character bento," where the foods in the boxes take on the shapes of anime characters, superheroes, animals, and other cute (*kawaii*) characters. They transform into works of art. I am amazed by the images of chara-ben I've found online, elaborate and beautiful boxes that moms put together for their children. It highlights a whole new level of obsession for me.

And yet, despite my deep, consuming, and endless love for my daughters . . . it doesn't extend to creating lunch art for them on a daily basis. For me, what resonates is the Japanese idea that when a person eats a box lunch prepared by a loved one, the preparer's feelings are transmitted through the food. The bento box is a vehicle for communication between the maker and the eater. In other words, my girls can feel the love and care that I put into making and packing their lunches through their boxes.

because of the higher cost of stainless steel. Plastic lids may have to be washed by hand, as they'll warp in the dishwasher. If hand washing is one more hassle you don't need, you may want to opt out of plastic.

If your decisions affected only you, you'd be ready to go forth now and buy a bento box or two. But we all know that our kids' habits and preferences play a huge role in what we actually spend our money on. So, square the info I just went through with these three key questions before buying anything:

IS YOUR KID GOING TO LOSE THE BOX ON THE SECOND DAY OF SCHOOL? Is that your kid, the one who somehow—innocently or not—misplaces everything? Then you'll probably want to opt for a cheaper box that is sold in packs. Likewise if your kiddo treats her lunch bag like a bat or ball.

DOES YOUR KID HAVE A SPECIAL LUNCH BAG IN WHICH YOU'LL PLACE—OR SHOVE— THE BENTO BOX? Ellie just *had* to have a blue lunch bag with whales on it for school. I actually found one and then had to keep the bag dimensions in mind for boxes that would fit.

DOES YOUR KIDDO PREFER GRAZING OR EATING ONE BIG MEAL? A large bento has many compartments and is great for those who prefer to eat everything at lunchtime. If your child tends to graze throughout the day, then two smaller boxes might work better than one bigger box—one for lunch and one for snack.

BENTO PACKING PRINCIPLES

You've got the bento box (or three), now how do you pack the darn thing? Having general guidelines to follow will make your lunch packing a little easier.

This book is going to give you tons of ideas for foods to pack, but here are two important considerations before we get to that:

How Much

How much you pack depends on your children's ages, how much they eat at lunch, and how many other snacks they have at school. One way I judge how much to pack is by how much food is sent home at the end of the day. If a ton of food comes home, then you might want to pack less of each food item. If the box is wiped clean, try adding more each day. You will also find that children's hunger, just like ours, varies from day to day; so, some days they will eat everything in sight and other days next to nothing. You can always turn the leftovers into an after-school snack.

Portions and Proportions

By this I mean which groups of food, and how much of each, to send every day. There's a general order in which I think through lunch:

PROTEIN / COMPLEX CARB / VEGGIE / FRUIT / TREAT

I start each box with a protein, so I know my girls will feel full and energized— chicken, yogurt, hardboiled eggs, seed or almond butter, and cheese are great places to start. Next I include complex carbohydrates found in foods such as whole-wheat bread, couscous, quinoa, tortillas, oatmeal, or granola. If the main recipe doesn't already have vegetables in it, I include some veggie sticks and dip. My girls love fruit, so I try to vary their intake from meal to meal—berries, apple slices, and melon balls are some of their favorites. Finally, I like to include a little treat, because lunches should be fun, too. This could be a homemade blueberry oatmeal cookie, fruit leather, party snack mix, a couple of dark chocolate chips in a cute container, or even a sweet note or drawing from me.

The United States Food and Drug Administration (FDA) has put together guidelines (check out choosemyplate.gov/kids) for the amounts and types of foods children need for the day. My "complex carb" category matches up to what the FDA lists as grains. For example, here are the recommended daily nutritional intakes for kids of varying ages:

Daily Nutritional Intake

Toddler	Preschooler	School-age	Teenager
2 ounces protein	4 ounces protein	5 ounces	5 ½ ounces protein
3 ounces grains (at least half should be whole grains)	5 ounces grains (at least half should be whole grains)	5 ounces grains (at least half should be whole grains)	6 ounces grain (at least half should be whole grains)
1 cup each fruits and vegetables	1 ½ cups each fruits and vegetables	2 cups each fruits and vegetables	2 ½ cups each fruits and vegetables
2 cups dairy	2 ½ cups dairy	3 cups dairy	3 cups dairy

These are not hard and fast rules, since every child is different and slight changes may be needed to best fit their nutritional likes and needs, not to mention their ages. Refer to these portion recommendations as you prepare the recipes for your bento boxes. Because I've stressed the importance of meal planning and making lunches from family meal leftovers, most recipes make far more than a single bento portion.

I ALSO WANT TO ADD A CAUTIONARY WORD about packing your bentos to match the photos featured in the chapters to come. The photos are there to entice your eyes and stomach and show you how the foods all fit together. I have packed these boxes to the brim so that you can really see everything. But keep in mind that the proportions in the photos are not 100 percent realistic in terms of what you would actually pack for your kid's lunch, particularly for the main dishes. Let the photos be an inspiration for what to pack in the bentos, and refer to the FDA's simple, straightforward guidelines for the recommended amounts.

MY BEST BENTO BUYS

Over time, I realized that the following bento boxes were the ones I reached for day in and day out. Don't think for a second that you need all of them. Not at all. Find the one that fits your life and go from there. While I showcase a variety of bentos in this book, you can easily make the recipes fit into whichever type of bento box works for you. For a full list of the boxes I used in this book, see Resources on page 167.

PLANETBOX ROVER OR SHUTTLE

The PlanetBox brand is the top tier of bento boxes. They are expensive, but their appealing design and perfectly portioned compartments make them a snap to fill and send to school. The Rover is great for older kids and adults, while the Shuttle is perfect for toddlers or younger kids.

What I Like

- The compartments are shallow, preventing me from packing too much food. The Rover has five compartments: one large main, three medium side/snack, and one small treat. The Shuttle has two compartments: one main and one side/snack.
- It is made from food-safe and dishwasher-safe materials.
- It won't retain yucky food odors or stains if you forget to wash it out for a week (it happens).
- The divided compartments prevent food from sliding and mixing.
- The Rover itself isn't leakproof, but it comes with two round (one big, one small) leakproof containers that fit nicely into the compartments.

What I Don't Like

- These are expensive. If your kids tend to lose everything, then this box is not for them.
- The decorative magnets have to be removed every time you wash the box.
- It will dent if your kid is rough with it.
- This is a small thing, but you will leave fingerprints on the box after assembling it.

PREMIUM BENTO LUNCH BOX CONTAINERS

These containers are one of our go-to boxes when packing for the entire family. They come in a pack of four and are just the right size for a toddler, kid, or smaller adult lunch. So, why don't you see these boxes in this book? There's a very simple reason: They don't photograph well. But you will see more photogenic three-compartment boxes that you can easily substitute with these if you find Premium is your style.

What I Like

- It is reasonably priced.
- It is made from food-safe materials.
- The containers and lids are microwave, dishwasher, and freezer safe.
- There are three compartments: one large main and two smaller side/snack sections.
- It has slightly rounded corners.
- It fits into almost all standard-size lunch bags.
- Older toddlers and kids can take off the lids themselves.

What I Don't Like

- Besides a colorful lid, there isn't much design to them.
- The compartments aren't completely leakproof, so they're not ideal for something as liquid as soup, but I do pack yogurt or pudding in the snack compartments.

INNOBABY DIN DIN SMART STAINLESS DIVIDED PLATTER WITH LID

What toddler wouldn't love this fun, bus-shaped bento? It's so cute! It features five smaller compartments to give your kids a variety of tastes.

What I Like

- It features two larger main and three snack-size containers.
- The divided compartments prevent food from sliding and mixing around.
- It is made from food-safe materials.
- The metal tray is dishwasher safe.
- It has slightly rounded corners.

What I Don't Like

- The lid is not dishwasher safe and must be hand washed so it won't warp.
- The bus shape is hard to fit into most standard-size lunch bags.
- It's not leakproof. But as with the Premium boxes, I have no problem sending yogurt in it.
- Sometimes it can be a challenge to fill all five compartments with different foods.

PACK THE RAINBOW

If there is only one thing that I hope you take away from this book, it's how many colors you can pack in a lunch. I fervently believe that colorful food is fun food. Colorful food is also naturally healthy food. Will your kids eat the entire rainbow in every bento? Probably not, but we can get close.

You don't need a nutrition degree to figure out how to make sure you pack foods with a variety of vitamins and minerals; nature makes it easy for anyone to do this. Fruits and veggies in different colors tend to be packed with different vitamins and minerals—it's as easy as that. Here's a brief summary:

> RED Most red fruits and vegetables have vitamin C. In addition, strawberries are high in folic acid, tomatoes have potassium, and red bell peppers are a great source of vitamin A.

> ORANGE AND YELLOW Here it's all about oranges, tangerines, carrots, and sweet potatoes, which are full of vitamin C, vitamin A, and beta-carotene.

> GREEN This is the be-all and end-all of healthy vegetables and fruits. Foods like broccoli, cabbage, asparagus, and kale are chock-full of vitamin K, folic acid, potassium, carotenoids, and omega-3 fatty acids. Green grapes and kiwi are high in fiber and vitamin K.

> BLUE/PURPLE Eating foods like blueberries, grapes, eggplant, and purple cabbage reduces the risk for high blood pressure and helps prevent obesity.

While the summer is certainly the most bountiful time for colorful food, every season has a wealth of fruits and vegetables to offer. For summer boxes, you can pack red watermelon, orange apricots, yellow bell pepper sticks, green avocado chunks, and blueberries or purple Concord grapes. For the winter months, try red pomegranate seeds, orange persimmon slices, roasted yellow squash, green broccoli, and blue plums or chopped purple carrots.

What about beige, you ask? Well, technically, beige is not a color of the rainbow. But the odds are pretty good that we'll pack some sort of beige food into our kids' lunches each day; this might be cheese, bread, grains, or hummus. The point is to offer a more varied diet then serving solely beige foods. Start with maybe one beige food as your base layer and then add as many colors to that as you can.

FOOD SAFETY

As concerning as food safety is and should be, packing your lunch to prevent food-borne illnesses is pretty easy and becomes second nature very quickly. There are three primary considerations:

TEMPERATURE OF FOOD The key is to keep cold foods cold and hot foods hot. Most lunch bags come with an ice pack, but if not, you can purchase one at most grocery stores or online. To keep hot foods hot, use an insulated thermos that is prepped properly. To do this, first fill it with hot or boiling water. Let it sit for 5 minutes, dump out the water, dry the interior of the thermos, put in the hot food, and seal immediately. This way foods meant to be hot will stay hot for up to 5 hours.

EVERYTHING BUT THE . . .

Some kids don't eat the meat, others don't eat the bread, some won't go near veggies with a ten-foot pole, and then there is the kid who eats only carrots—go figure. Let's face it, kids are weird! One of my major challenges with my girls' eating habits is that neither of them likes to eat bread, waffles, or pancakes. Parker won't even go near cookies or cake (seriously, something must be wrong there).

But that shouldn't stop us trying to feed our children a healthy and well-rounded meal. Because one day they will turn into normal humans and eat more than just the carrots, or the cookies. Hopefully, with a little coaxing and possibly some strategic bribing, we can get them to eat a variety of foods.

Here are some recipes to try for those "picky" eaters:

Doesn't like bread? Try the Deconstructed Cobb Salad (page 129), Italian Turkey Meatballs (page 81), or Spinach + Cheese Quiches (page 53).

Doesn't like chicken (or tofu)? Try the Curried Chickpea Salad (page 99), Carrot + Beet Cream Cheese Sandwiches (page 101), or Coconut Rice with Snap Peas + Edamame (page 69).

Doesn't like the veg? Try the Veggie-Loaded Pepperoni Pizza Rollups (page 59), Kid-Friendly Veggie Chili with the veggies blended (page 73), or Roasted Carrot + Cumin Hummus (page 41).

Doesn't like the fruit? Try the Overnight Strawberry Chia Seed Pudding (page 39), Simply Spiced Applesauce (page 47), or Raspberry + Lemon Fruit Leather (page 106).

CLEAN WELL The first step, which is sometimes harder than it seems, is to make sure your kids actually bring home their bento box every day. Then make sure you wash and dry the box after each use with hot soapy water or in the dishwasher. A wipe with a wet paper towel or washcloth, no matter how thorough, won't do.

WHEN IN DOUBT, TOSS IT OUT I love serving Ellie's lunch leftovers to her for a late-afternoon snack. But sometimes I open her bento box in the afternoon and don't even know what happened during the day—the food is in one big pile of gloop or something just doesn't smell right anymore. Usually foods that don't need to be heated or chilled are fine for a quick snack option—fruit, crackers, carrot sticks, dried fruit, and so on. But after I pick through the box for snack items, everything else goes into the compost bin.

PLANNING AHEAD TO KEEP MORNING PREP SANE

I'm not sure what happens at your house in the morning, but mine is pretty much chaos. Kids half-dressed, refusing to brush their hair until every toy car in the house is put in a choo-choo line that goes out of their room and down the hall, all the while the breakfast is burning, or getting cold, or not being made at all. It feels as though most days we barely make it out of the door clothed, fed, and in one piece. So, if trying to wrap your head around making a fun and healthy lunch just might make it explode, I hear you!

After some experimenting, I have learned some tricks for a smoother lunch-making process (and life in general). Don't worry—you don't have to follow all these strategies every week. Start with one, give it a go, and then make it work into your family's life:

PLAN IT OUT Make a menu plan for the week that includes lunches and dinners. If you're super type A like me, jot down some breakfast ideas as well. I tend to write down breakfast meals, but I find that I often don't stick to them, instead just tossing together whatever I have on hand. Lunch and dinner are different, though. If I write it down, I do it. And having a cute meal planner never hurts. On page 24, I give a meal planner you can use (which you can also download at babyfoode.com/mealplanner).

When I plan a week's worth of dinners, I keep in mind leftovers for lunch. I post the meal plan right on the wall next to our refrigerator, so my husband can start dinner when I am not home. Yes, really!

LOVE YOUR LEFTOVERS Where would we be without leftovers? They are the key to saving time. One category of leftovers is meals that can be reused as is. For example, I love to make a big pot of soup, a grain salad, or a big batch of lasagna or enchiladas. Then, during the week, I can reuse the same meal as is. Done and done. For other meals, I repurpose the leftovers into other meals. Leftover grilled chicken can be turned into chicken salad, roasted vegetables become a topping on pita pizzas, and the pesto sauce I used in a pasta dish is saved to spread on grilled cheese sandwiches.

USE YOUR FREEZER Your freezer is your friend; it isn't just the appliance that gets your beer cold in 9 minutes, so use it to your advantage. Make a double batch of your kids' favorite pizza rolls, waffles, muffins, cookies, pasta sauce, and even smoothies, and freeze the extra so you always have something on hand.

PREP AHEAD OF TIME Many people love to do a big weekend prep of everything they are going to need for the busy week ahead. The idea is you chop, dice, and make simple dishes so you have them all ready when you need them. If this fits your style, I recommend you check out TheLeanGreenBean.com, which offers a ton of organizational planning tips. As for me, I can't commit to spending my weekends this way. I'm fortunate that as a work-from-home mom, I can usually start dinner prep during lunchtime. I put the bento on the counter right away. That way when I chop-up bell peppers for taco night, I can easily make some bell pepper sticks to dip into hummus at the same time. I usually prep some of the bento items during dinner prep and finish it off right before dinner cleanup.

Now, I have no expectation that you are going to pack your kid's lunch every day with three made-from-scratch recipes. Real life just doesn't allow it, and we all recognize and need to be okay with that. I didn't write this book with the thought that you would or should put that much time into your lunch making. I put these boxes together to show you the different options that are out there, realizing that you would save your sanity and fill one, or maybe two, of the bento compartments with a homemade recipe and complete the box with cut fruit and veggies, cheese, yogurt, dips, or other super simple ingredients that take zero prep time.

THIS WEEK'S MEALS

	Breakfast	Lunch	Dinner
Sunday			
Monday			
Tuesday			
Wednesday			
Thursday			
Friday			
Saturday			

A MINIMUM OF SUPPORTING EQUIPMENT

Besides the actual bento box, there aren't many other tools you need to make a healthy, delectable lunch for your child. Most supporting equipment and accessories are just for aesthetics, so don't let the following list put you off. You can gather these items as you go along, or not at all. Most of the accessories are very affordable, ranging from $4 to $8 per item. I like to pick up something new every few months to keep the boxes fresh. I get almost all my bento accessories online, but if you feel up for some kitchen eye candy, a trip to your local Japanese or Asian market will surely result in some great bento and food treasures. In addition to Resources (page 167), you can find a complete list of my favorite brands of bento boxes and accessories on my blog.

Must Have

❭ THERMOS Having a thermos on hand, especially during the colder months, is crucial for sending warm foods to school. I find that a wide-mouth thermos jar is easiest for kids to eat out of.

❭ ICE PACK Some bentos come with an ice pack, or you can pick up one separately. I recommend keeping it in the freezer at all times, so it's nice and cold when you need to pack it in a bento to keep certain foods cold.

❭ WATER BOTTLE I love the water bottles from Klean Kanteen and CamelBak.

❭ SPOON/FORK Pack a utensil that you are okay losing. Chances are these utensils will make it home only about half of the time.

Nice to Have

❭ SILICONE MUFFIN CUPS These come in a variety of shapes and colors. Even though they are intended to be used as muffin liners, I have never actually made muffins in them. Instead, I put treats or snacks in them. The girls also love to use them to store their newest treasures in (aka painted rocks).

❭ KEBAB SKEWERS AND/OR LOLLIPOP STICKS Kids love eating anything and everything on a stick, so I always have a stash of wooden kebab skewers or paper lollipop sticks in my kitchen. The skewers are easy to cut into the size you want; just make sure you cut off the pointy end so your kid doesn't poke herself (or her lunch buddy). The lollipop sticks are great for younger kids because they are thicker and easier to hold onto.

❭ BENTO OR COOKIE CUTTERS Cutters come in a range of shapes and designs. Bento cutters are usually a simple shape in two different sizes, and they can cut easily through vegetables. Cookie cutters are generally bigger but are not great for cutting through harder food. When I started making Ellie's bento boxes, I used old (but clean) Play-Doh cutters!

> MELON BALLER It's so circa 1954, but the melon baller is a cheap kitchen gadget that makes watermelon, melon, mango, and avocado so much more fun.

> SMALL ROUND CONTAINERS WITH LIDS These small containers are great for dipping sauces, dressing, or a small treat. They usually come in a four-pack of fun colors and designs.

> BIGGER ROUND CONTAINERS WITH LIDS These are especially nice to have if your bento box compartments are not leakproof. You can usually find these in stainless steel with a colorful lid.

In this book certain recipes call for kebab skewers, cutters, or a rolling pin. This doesn't mean that you need any of these items. No cutters? Use a knife to cut food into squares or triangles. No skewers? Just don't use them. My items and designs are just to give you ideas; adjust them based on your time, budget, and what you already have.

BREAK YOUR RULES (AND MINE)

We're all human and we all have our limitations. Once in a while, we all reach for a bag of veggie sticks instead of fresh vegetables. And as much as I love cooking, I will absolutely allow myself a break from the relentless pressure to eat clean and make everything from scratch. Truth is, kids like a bit of change, too. Especially if that change tastes sweet.

Dried fruits, nuts (if your school allows), and seeds are almost so obvious it's easy to forget them. Keep in mind that they can be high in natural sugar or fat, so small serving sizes are important. Here are some of our favorites:

DRIED FRUITS apples, apricots, bananas, blueberries, cherries, cranberries, currants, golden raisins, mango, pineapple, raisins, strawberries

SHELLED NUTS AND SEEDS almonds, cashews, pecans, pepitas (pumpkin seeds), pistachios, sunflower seeds

There are also the—gulp—premade foods my kids and I have a weakness for, too. They don't show up at lunch every day, but they definitely make the occasional appearance, and I don't let it bother me one bit:

CRUNCHY/SALTY Cheddar Bunnies, crackers, crunchy dry cereal or granola, kettle chips, pretzels, seaweed snacks, sesame sticks, Snapea Crisps, Veggie Straws

SWEET chocolate-covered anything (almonds, sunflower seeds, pretzels, raisins), fruit chews, graham crackers, mini cookies, yogurt-covered raisins or pretzels

HAPPY, HEALTHY EATERS THROUGHOUT THE YEAR

This book is organized seasonally, beginning in the fall when we typically send the kiddos off to school and ending in the summer. I organized the book this way for ease of use but also because while it might be easiest to put together a bento in the summer when the produce choices seem limitless, kids still need to eat all year long. This book serves up inspiration no matter which month, no matter what's in season. But just because I put these boxes into seasons doesn't mean that you can't use them all year long. They are made to be able to easily transition from season to season with only a few simple ingredient switches, if any.

BENTO BOXES AND RECIPES—WITH OPTIONS!

Here's the rundown on how this book is presented. Each recipe chapter has photos of eight composed bento boxes, with a main, side, and either a snack or special treat. Not everything in each box requires a recipe, but following each photo are recipes for the main and the side.

Some boxes offer a recipe for an "alternative main," which you won't see pictured in the box. The alternative might be vegetarian if the main isn't, or it might be a radical flavor twist on the main in the box. The point is to give you options.

Each chapter ends with a "Quick Bento" for those days when you need to pack something healthy and satisfying with minimal preparation.

Dietary labels let you know if a recipe is—or includes an ingredient option that would make it—dairy free, gluten free, nut free, vegetarian (veg), or vegan.

What I'd really love is for you to have fun making your kids' lunches instead of viewing it as a laborious task. Even though you are not there to see them open up their thoughtfully composed lunch, your kiddos are going to realize and appreciate the love and care you took to make it—even if they never say a word. The greatest compliment is an empty bento.

EASY MEALS ANY TIME OF YEAR

We all have those times when we forget (read: are too tired) to pack a lunch the night before, our early morning workout runs late, or we "forget" to set our alarm and only get up when we hear the kids in the bathroom and it is *way* too quiet in there for anything good to be happening. At these times, we don't stand a chance of putting together a composed bento, but we can still dash off a quick, easy, and nutritious main meal. Here are my four go-to recipes for days like these. If you're pressed for time and have some fresh fruit or chopped veggies on hand, pair them with these mains and you've made a balanced meal in just 5 or 10 minutes.

If these ideas resonate with you, check out the final bento of each chapter, which I've called "Quick Bentos." These include 10-minutes-or-less mains and virtually no-prep sides for each season, using ingredients you most likely have in your kitchen already. I'm betting you'll come back to these simple lunches again and again—I know I do!

PANCAKE + JAM SANDWICH

I make double batches of pancakes on the weekends so I always have some in the freezer for easy morning breakfasts. This means that making a sweet pancake sandwich is a fun and fast way to turn breakfast into lunch. If you don't have homemade pancakes at your beck and call, you can easily use store-bought frozen pancakes or waffles—just make sure to toast or microwave them before assembling.

Spread 2 teaspoons cream cheese onto a 6-inch pancake and 1 teaspoon of your favorite jam on another pancake (roughly the same shape). Press the pancakes together to make a sandwich and serve whole or cut into wedges. You can also use a cookie cutter and cut it into your kid's favorite shape.

GRAHAM CRACKER + BLUEBERRY GOAT CHEESE SANDWICHES

Trader Joe's sells a blueberry goat cheese log I can't buy because my family will sit on the kitchen floor like a pack of wild animals and devour the entire thing in 5 minutes flat. It's that good. So instead, I make it one sandwich at a time. It helps with portion control and our dining manners.

In a small microwave-safe bowl, combine 2 tablespoons goat cheese (cream cheese or any other spreadable cheese will also work) and 1 tablespoon blueberry jam (or any other jam your kids like). Microwave for 10 seconds—just until the goat cheese is soft enough to spread. Mix the goat cheese and jam and spread the mixture onto two full graham cracker sheets. Top with two more graham cracker sheets and gently break them into eight pieces, following the graham cracker seams.

BANANA + PEANUT BUTTER ROLLUP WITH CINNAMON + HONEY

Long name, simple recipe. I saw a cute recipe on Pinterest and knew I had to try it. It was good but needed a little something extra, so I added a pinch of cinnamon and a drizzle of honey to turn this into one of my girls' favorite rollups.

Spread 1 tablespoon peanut butter (or any nut or seed butter) over the entire surface of a medium or large tortilla. Make sure to spread all the way to the edges—this makes for a "glue" so the tortilla stays together when you roll it up. Sprinkle on ¼ teaspoon ground cinnamon and drizzle 2 teaspoons honey over the peanut butter. Peel a banana and place it in the middle of the tortilla. Tightly roll the tortilla around the banana. Cut into 1-inch-thick pinwheels.

BITS + PIECES LUNCH

Here's what to do when you have absolutely nothing in your fridge. The inspiration is a delicious charcuterie platter with meats, cheese, bites of fruit, and maybe even some chocolate. The reality is you are just taking anything you have left in the kitchen and transforming it into a lunch. I love packing each item in a baby food purée container (since I have a million lying around), but you can use small jars or cupcake holders for each item.

Items that I have used include sliced lunch meat or salami, leftover chicken or beef, slices or hunks of any kind of cheese, edamame, red pepper slices, pomegranate seeds, grapes, blackberries, dried cranberries, mandarin oranges, crackers, chocolate-covered raisins, and even granola.

2

Fall

Fall is one of my favorite times to make, bake, and eat warm, comforting, and healthy foods. In my house, fall means classic comfort foods such as hearty soups, grilled cheese sandwiches, homemade applesauce, and straight-out-of-the-oven cookies. It's a season that fills our kitchens and our stomachs with the taste and smell of earthy, spiced flavors. While it does take a little more time to prep and pack warm items in a bento lunch, the payoff is sending your children to school with satisfying foods that will fuel them through the cooler days.

BENTO 1

A kale quesadilla? In a kid's lunch? Absolutely. This is a complete winner in our house—even my husband gives it a big thumbs-up. Kale, while super nutritious, is hard to market to the kiddos (and husbands), mostly because of its sometimes-tough texture. My solution is to blend the kale into a pesto of sorts, with a little sweet apple, cheese, and garlic, then smear it on a tortilla with a bit more cheese and cook until it has the perfect crispy and gooey combination that we all crave from our favorite quesadilla. Paired with a warm and creamy Thai pumpkin soup and a delicious but wholesome oat cookie—what better way could there be to meet the cool, crisp fall days?

Cheesy Kale Quesadillas

3 kale leaves, stemmed and roughly chopped (about 2 cups)

½ apple, peeled, cored, chopped

1 garlic clove, peeled

1½ cups mozzarella or sharp white Cheddar cheese, divided

1 tablespoon extra-virgin olive oil, plus 1 teaspoon

Salt

Freshly ground black pepper

4 large tortillas (white, whole-wheat, or gluten-free)

SERVES 2

STORAGE
3 days in refrigerator

PREP TIME
5 minutes
COOK TIME
12 to 15 minutes

veg

nut free

gluten free

In a food processor or blender, combine the kale, apple, garlic, ½ cup of cheese, 1 tablespoon of olive oil, salt, and pepper. Blend, scraping down the sides of the bowl if needed, until everything is combined and resembles a chunky pesto, 30 to 60 seconds.

Heat the remaining 1 teaspoon of olive oil in a medium skillet over medium heat. Spread roughly 2 tablespoons of the kale pesto onto one tortilla, sprinkle ¼ cup of cheese over the kale, and cover it with another tortilla. Place the quesadilla in the skillet and cook until golden brown, about 3 minutes. Flip it and cook for another 2 to 3 minutes. Repeat this step with the remaining tortillas, kale mixture, and cheese. You will have 2 quesadillas.

Let the quesadillas cool on a cutting board for 5 minutes. Cut each into 4 wedges and serve. If packing for lunch, let cool completely before placing in the bento box.

SUBSTITUTION TIP: This recipe also works great if you use sweet potatoes instead of kale. They make for a wonderful sweet and savory taste, and I love to add some rinsed and drained canned black beans and a sprinkle of chopped red onion to these quesadillas. Simply peel and roughly chop 1 small cooked sweet potato and add it and ½ teaspoon ground cumin to the blender. Blend and cook as directed above.

Quick + Creamy Thai Pumpkin Soup

SERVES 6

FREEZER FRIENDLY

STORAGE
1 week in refrigerator, 2 months in freezer

PREP TIME
5 minutes
COOK TIME
10 minutes

vegan

nut free

dairy free

gluten free

1 tablespoon extra-virgin olive oil

½ onion, roughly chopped

1 garlic clove, roughly chopped

½ teaspoon ground cumin

½ teaspoon ground ginger

1 teaspoon red curry paste

1 (15-ounce) can pumpkin purée

1 tablespoon tomato paste

2 cups vegetable or chicken broth

1 cup canned coconut milk

Salt

Freshly ground black pepper

In a medium stockpot, heat the oil over medium heat. Add the onion and sauté until almost soft and translucent, about 3 minutes. Add the garlic and sauté for 1 minute. Stir in the cumin, ginger, and red curry paste and cook for 1 minute.

Transfer the onion mixture to a blender and add the pumpkin purée, tomato paste, broth, and coconut milk. Blend on high until completely smooth, 2 to 3 minutes.

Return the soup to the stockpot and bring it just to a boil. Season with salt and pepper and serve. If packing for lunch, the soup will stay warm in a thermos for about 5 hours.

MAKE IT A MEAL: To make this soup into a hearty meal, double the recipe. Once the soup comes to a boil, add 1½ cups fresh cheese tortellini, 1 cup finely shredded fresh spinach, and 2 diced tomatoes. Continue to cook until the tortellini is cooked through, about 7 minutes, adding an additional cup of broth if needed. Serve with Crunchy Moroccan-Spiced Chickpeas (page 111) for dinner or pack in a thermos for a hot lunch.

Blueberry + Oat Cookies

½ cup coconut oil or unsalted butter, at room temperature

¼ cup brown sugar

¼ cup granulated sugar

1 large egg

1 teaspoon pure vanilla extract

1 cup white whole-wheat flour

½ teaspoon ground cinnamon

¼ teaspoon baking soda

¼ teaspoon baking powder

¼ teaspoon salt

1 cup old-fashioned oats

1 cup dried blueberries

MAKES
18 COOKIES

FREEZER
FRIENDLY

STORAGE
1 week in
airtight
container,
2 months in
freezer

PREP TIME
15 minutes
COOK TIME
15 minutes

veg

nut
free

dairy
free

Preheat the oven to 350°F.

In the bowl of a standing mixer, cream the coconut oil and sugars on high until fluffy, 1 to 2 minutes. Add the egg and vanilla extract and beat for another minute, scraping down the sides of the bowl if needed.

In a medium bowl, sift together the flour, cinnamon, baking soda, baking powder, and salt. Incorporate the dry ingredients into the wet ingredients and mix until just combined. Add the oats and mix until just combined. Add the dried blueberries and mix until just combined.

Spoon 1 tablespoon of dough onto a baking sheet for each cookie, placing the cookies about 2 inches apart. Bake until golden brown on the bottom, 12 to 15 minutes. Let the cookies cool on the baking sheet for 2 minutes, then transfer to a wire rack to cool completely.

INGREDIENT TIP: Dried blueberries can be quite expensive, so I always stock up on them when they go on sale. If you can't find them or they aren't on sale, or if you just want to mix things up a bit, try dried cranberries, dried cherries, or raisins.

The first time I had Mexican street corn was at a trendy little restaurant in Oakland, California. I ate it with such vigor I'm pretty sure our table neighbors were impressed (or possibly grossed out) by my dedication to eating every single delicious kernel on the cob. This is my healthy take on that dish—a simple, almost-but-not-quite burnt corn mixed with yogurt, garlic, chili powder, and a sprinkle of cotija cheese. The corn goes perfectly with the crispy baked beef taquitos. Serve both with a big side of my Easy-Peasy Guacamole (page 161) to round out the Mexican food theme, and add a serving of strawberry chia pudding for a slightly sweet treat.

Baked Beef Taquitos

Cooking spray

2 teaspoons extra-virgin olive oil

1 pound lean ground beef

2 tablespoons water

2 tablespoons chili powder

1 teaspoon onion powder

1 teaspoon ground cumin

½ teaspoon garlic powder

½ teaspoon paprika

½ teaspoon salt

¼ teaspoon freshly ground black pepper

12 medium tortillas (white, whole-wheat, or gluten-free)

2 cups shredded sharp Cheddar cheese or Mexican cheese blend

MAKES 12 TAQUITOS

FREEZER FRIENDLY

STORAGE
4 days in refrigerator, 2 months in freezer

PREP TIME
15 minutes
COOK TIME
20 minutes

nut free

gluten free

Preheat the oven to 425°F. Coat a baking sheet with cooking spray.

Heat the olive oil in a large skillet over medium-high heat, then add the beef and cook, stirring often, until the beef is in crumbles, 7 to 10 minutes. Drain if needed.

Add the water, chili powder, onion powder, cumin, garlic powder, paprika, salt, and pepper, and stir until well combined. Remove the skillet from the heat.

If the tortillas are hard to roll without breaking, warm them slightly in the microwave or oven. Spread a heaping tablespoon of the beef mixture in a line down the middle of one tortilla. Top it with a heaping tablespoon of the shredded cheese, then sprinkle a little more cheese over the rest of the tortilla to help it stick better once it is rolled.

Tightly roll up the tortilla and place it on the baking sheet. If it won't stay rolled, use a toothpick to hold it together while baking. Repeat with the remaining tortillas.

Spray each taquito with cooking spray. Bake for 7 minutes, flip, and continue baking until crispy and brown, another 3 to 5 minutes. Let cool for a few minutes before serving. If packing for lunch, cool completely before placing in the bento box.

SUBSTITUTION TIP: This recipe works just as well with ground turkey, ground chicken, soy crumbles, or a can of rinsed and drained black beans. If you're using beans, they only need to be heated through with the spices. Any leftover meat or bean mixture is great to use in quesadillas later in the week for lunch or as a quick add-in to scrambled eggs in the morning.

Mexican Street Corn

1 tablespoon extra-virgin olive oil

3 ears corn, kernels cut off the cobs, or
1 cup frozen corn, thawed

3 tablespoons plain Greek yogurt or
sour cream, 2% or full-fat

Juice of ½ lime

1 garlic clove, minced

¼ teaspoon chili powder

Salt

Freshly ground black pepper

3 tablespoons cotija cheese,
shredded or crumbled

Heat the oil in a skillet over medium-high heat. Add the corn and cook, stirring occasionally, until most of the kernels are golden brown and some are just starting to burn, 7 to 10 minutes. You will want some pieces of the corn to be slightly charred.

In a small bowl, stir together the yogurt, lime juice, garlic, chili powder, salt, and pepper.

Remove the skillet from the heat and stir in the yogurt sauce until well combined. Sprinkle with the cheese and serve. If packing for lunch, cool completely before placing in the bento box.

SUBSTITUTION TIP: If you can't find cotija cheese, substitute feta or Romano cheese.

MAKE IT A MEAL: I am not joking when I say you will want to eat this corn at every meal for the next week. To turn this side into a full-scale meal, toss the finished corn with 1½ cups cooked quinoa, 2 sliced scallions, 1 cup chopped cherry tomatoes, ½ cup rinsed and drained canned black beans, and ½ chopped avocado. Drizzle with an additional 2 tablespoons extra-virgin olive oil and sprinkle an additional 3 tablespoons cheese on top. You can also add 1 cup diced cooked chicken or steak to the top or add this mega corn mixture to a bed of fresh greens. For a fun kick, my husband and I like a little hot sauce drizzled over the top, too.

Overnight Strawberry Chia Seed Pudding

1 cup strawberries, fresh or frozen
and thawed

1 banana

¼ cup canned coconut milk

¼ cup honey

1 teaspoon pure vanilla extract

¼ cup chia seeds

SERVES 4

STORAGE
3 days in
refrigerator

PREP TIME
5 minutes
CHILL TIME
2 to 12 hours

veg

nut
free

dairy
free

gluten
free

In a blender or food processor, blend the strawberries, banana, coconut milk, honey, and vanilla extract on high speed until creamy and smooth, 30 to 60 seconds.

Transfer to a bowl and stir in the chia seeds. Cover the bowl and refrigerate overnight so the pudding sets and chills.

Serve the pudding as is, or for a smooth pudding, blend it for 60 to 90 seconds on high speed until the chia seeds are completely puréed. If packing for lunch, use an ice pack.

PREP TIP: It's important that the pudding sets and chills before you eat it, but the truth is that it doesn't really need 12 or more hours for this. You can dive into this pudding after just 2 hours of chilling. I call this an overnight pudding because there's no way I'm getting up at 4:00 a.m. to make sure it has enough time to chill before going into the bento.

INGREDIENT TIP: I could add coconut to any dish and be just fine with it. This pudding is amazing with ¼ cup shredded coconut added after blending. You can also add a sprinkle of coconut on top right before serving if you want to give it a really finished look.

Hummus with pita chips and cut veggies is my go-to lunch for Ellie when I am short on time in the morning. Most weekends I make a batch of hummus and have it ready in the fridge for the crazy week ahead. I find that I use it just as much for my own lunches when I am on the go and don't have time for an actual meal. What makes this lunch extra special is sending crispy toasted spiced pita chips and a soft, decadent whole-wheat coconut cookie, along with the veggies, fresh clementine segments, and some dried fruit. And while I would love to eat a cookie after lunch, it's a certainty I'll have already eaten mine with my morning cup of coffee.

Roasted Carrot + Cumin Hummus

Cooking spray

2 medium carrots, roughly chopped

¼ cup extra-virgin olive oil, plus
2 teaspoons, and more for serving

½ teaspoon paprika, plus more
for serving

1 (15-ounce) can chickpeas

1 garlic clove, peeled

Juice of 1 lemon

1 teaspoon ground cumin

½ teaspoon ground ginger

Salt

Freshly ground black pepper

**MAKES
2 CUPS**

STORAGE
1 week in
refrigerator

PREP TIME
5 minutes
COOK TIME
30 minutes

vegan

nut
free

dairy
free

gluten
free

Preheat the oven to 450°F. Coat a baking sheet with cooking spray or line it with a silicone mat.

Spread out the carrots on the baking sheet in a single layer. Drizzle them with 2 teaspoons of olive oil and sprinkle with the paprika. Roast the carrots until tender, about 30 minutes.

Drain ⅓ cup liquid from the canned chickpeas and discard it.

Combine the roasted carrots, chickpeas with remaining liquid, garlic, lemon juice, cumin, ginger, salt, and pepper in a food processor or blender, and pulse until the ingredients are well mixed.

With the machine running on full speed, slowly drizzle in the remaining ¼ cup of olive oil and blend until the hummus is smooth and creamy, 1 to 2 minutes.

Spoon the hummus into a bowl and drizzle with more olive oil and a sprinkle of paprika. If adding to a bento, spoon about 2 tablespoons into a small container.

MAKE IT A MEAL: This hummus makes an awesome spread for the best vegetarian sandwich: Take two slices of thick-cut bread or ciabatta and spread 2 heaping tablespoons of hummus on one slice and mayonnaise on the other; then layer on 2 thick avocado slices, 2 thick tomato slices, 6 thin cucumber slices, and a handful of fresh baby greens, then top with a slice of Gouda or pepper Jack cheese, a dash of freshly ground black pepper, and 2 pickles. Serve with Baked Sweet Potato Chips (page 102) and a warm cookie.

Toasted Spiced Pita Chips

SERVES 12

STORAGE
4 days in partially open container

PREP TIME
5 minutes
COOK TIME
15 minutes

veg

nut free

dairy free

Cooking spray

6 large pitas (whole-wheat or white)

¼ cup extra-virgin olive oil

1 teaspoon paprika

½ teaspoon garlic powder

¼ teaspoon onion powder

Salt

Preheat the oven to 375°F.

Spray a baking sheet with cooking spray or line with aluminum foil or a silicone mat. Cut each pita into 8 wedges and place on the baking sheet.

In a small bowl, mix the oil, paprika, garlic powder, and onion powder. Brush the top of the pita wedges with the oil mixture, sprinkle with a bit of salt, and bake until crispy and golden brown, 12 to 15 minutes.

Let cool before serving. If packing into a bento box or storage container, let them cool completely—this helps them stay crisp. I have also found that not shutting the storage container lid completely helps maintain their crispiness.

BONUS RECIPE: I also love these pita chips as soup dippers. To pair with the Quick + Creamy Thai Pumpkin Soup (page 34), bake the pita wedges with a mixture of ¼ cup extra-virgin olive oil, ½ teaspoon garlic powder, ½ teaspoon dried thyme, and ¼ teaspoon ground cumin, then sprinkle with salt.

Whole-Wheat Coconut Cookies

½ cup shredded coconut

1 cup white whole-wheat flour

½ teaspoon baking soda

½ teaspoon baking powder

½ teaspoon salt

½ cup unsalted butter or coconut oil, at room temperature

⅓ cup brown sugar

¼ cup granulated sugar

1 large egg

½ teaspoon pure vanilla extract

½ cup white chocolate chips

Preheat the oven to 350°F.

Spread out the coconut on a baking sheet in a single layer and toast, stirring occasionally, until golden brown, 7 to 10 minutes. Set aside to cool.

In a medium bowl, whisk together the flour, baking soda, baking powder, and salt.

In another medium bowl or in a stand mixer, cream the butter and sugars until light and fluffy. Add the egg and the vanilla extract and mix until combined, scraping down the sides of the bowl if needed. On low speed, slowly mix in the flour mixture until just combined. Gently mix in the white chocolate chips and toasted coconut.

For mini cookies, drop or roll the dough onto the baking sheet in 1-teaspoon mounds. For regular-size cookies, drop or roll the dough onto the baking sheet in 1-tablespoon mounds.

Bake until golden brown, 8 to 10 minutes. Cool for 2 minutes on the baking sheet and then transfer to a wire rack to cool completely.

INGREDIENT TIP: Feel free to add ½ cup chopped macadamia nuts to these cookies for a truly tropical-inspired treat. Aloha!

Serving a regular salad to most kids is just not going to happen. Lettuce is a hard sell. But I love making a huge salad for
myself for lunch or dinner. One night, instead of making a
separate meal for the girls, I just ran with offering them the
same salad I was eating but deconstructed it for them, serving everything but the lettuce along with a "dipping sauce"
(dressing). They were in love. An entire plate of food that they
just *had* to dunk into a fun dipping sauce? Sold! Apples are at their height of
deliciousness in the fall, so a simple applesauce is the perfect side to usher in
the season. If you don't have enough time to make homemade, organic prepared applesauce is easy to buy. This bento is completed with a popcorn recipe
you'll definitely want to prep (and snack on) the night before.

Deconstructed Strawberry + Roasted Squash Salad

FOR THE SALAD

Cooking spray

1 medium butternut squash, seeded, peeled, and cubed (about 4 cups)

1 tablespoon extra-virgin olive oil

½ teaspoon salt

½ teaspoon freshly ground black pepper

1 avocado, pitted, peeled, and chopped

3 cups cubed cooked chicken

2 cups quartered strawberries

2 cups croutons, store-bought or homemade (page 161)

1 cup sharp white Cheddar cheese cubes

8 cups mixed greens (for the adults)

FOR THE DIPPING SAUCE

½ cup plain Greek yogurt, 2% or full-fat

3 tablespoons extra-virgin olive oil

3 tablespoons apple cider vinegar

2 tablespoons honey

2 teaspoons Dijon mustard

½ teaspoon salt

1 tablespoon poppy seeds

SERVES 6

STORAGE
2 days in refrigerator

PREP TIME
15 minutes
COOK TIME
30 minutes

nut free

Preheat the oven to 400°F. Coat a baking sheet with cooking spray.

Spread out the butternut squash in a single layer on the baking sheet. Drizzle it with the olive oil and sprinkle with the salt and pepper. Toss with your hands until the squash is evenly coated. Roast the squash until fork-tender, 25 to 30 minutes. If making croutons (page 161), do it while the squash roasts.

In a small bowl, make the dipping sauce by whisking together the Greek yogurt, olive oil, vinegar, honey, mustard, and salt until creamy and smooth. Add the poppy seeds and stir until blended. Stir the dipping sauce again before using as the poppy seeds tend to fall to the bottom of the container over time.

To assemble the salad on a plate or in a bento box, line up the roasted butternut squash, avocado, chicken, strawberries, croutons, and cheese. Serve with a small container of the dipping sauce. For the adults, line up the ingredients over a big bed of mixed greens and drizzle with the dipping sauce.

BENTO PACKING TIP: When putting together a school lunch, I pack everything the night before except the croutons and the avocado. The morning of, I add the croutons to the bento box, along with the avocado, chopped fresh, with a squeeze from half a lemon or lime to keep the avocado from browning.

Crazy Addicting Peanut Butter + Cinnamon Popcorn

¼ cup honey

2 tablespoons sugar

¼ cup creamy peanut butter

½ teaspoon pure vanilla extract

½ teaspoon ground cinnamon

6 cups air-popped popcorn

½ teaspoon sea salt

STORAGE
1 week in airtight container

PREP TIME
5 minutes
COOK TIME
5 minutes
COOL TIME
1 hour

veg

dairy free

gluten free

In a small saucepan, heat the honey and sugar over medium-low heat, stirring until dissolved. Add the peanut butter and stir until dissolved. Add the vanilla extract and cinnamon and stir until the mixture is creamy and smooth.

In a large bowl or clean brown paper bag, combine the popcorn and the peanut butter sauce. Toss until the popcorn is evenly coated.

Spread out the popcorn in an even layer on a baking sheet, sprinkle with the salt, and let cool for at least 1 hour. The flavors really start to come out when the popcorn is completely cool.

INGREDIENT TIP: Any smooth nut or seed butter—almond, cashew, sunflower seed—works great with this recipe. If your child's school is nut-free, try using Seed Butter (page 77) and adding up to ½ teaspoon more cinnamon to the butter mix before pouring it over the popcorn. I find that cashew and seed butter need just a little extra spice to give them more flavor.

Simply Spiced Applesauce

8 apples, peeled, cored, and roughly chopped

½ teaspoon ground cinnamon

⅛ teaspoon ground nutmeg

⅛ teaspoon ground cloves

1 cup water

FREEZER FRIENDLY

STORAGE
1 week in refrigerator, 2 months in freezer

PREP TIME:
10 minutes
COOK TIME
30 minutes

vegan

nut free

dairy free

gluten free

In a large stockpot, combine all the ingredients. Bring to a boil, reduce the heat to low, cover, and simmer, stirring occasionally, until the apples are tender, about 30 minutes.

For a chunky applesauce, break the larger apple chunks apart with the back of a wooden spoon or potato masher. For a smooth applesauce, transfer the mixture to a blender and purée for 1 minute. Serve warm or cold. If packing in a bento, the applesauce should be cold.

INGREDIENT TIP: My favorite apples for applesauce are Fuji, McIntosh, Jonagold, Golden Delicious, and Gala. I usually use a mix of whatever I have in the fridge when applesauce inspiration hits me. For a fun twist on this classic applesauce, add 10 large frozen strawberries and ½ teaspoon pure vanilla extract to the pot when cooking the apples. This strawberry applesauce is a fun and bright way to surprise your little one's taste buds.

Who says oatmeal can only be eaten in the morning hours? Oatmeal makes for a wonderfully hearty meal, and no kid will think twice about putting it away at lunchtime. This DIY oatmeal with add-ins is a great, fast lunch to make when time is of the essence. The core ingredients go in the thermos; the oats cook and are kept warm for the entire day. Muffins are something I pretty much always have a stash of in my freezer for when I need a quick lunch addition (or a quick breakfast), and these spiced carrot muffins are perfect for such an occasion. When packed in a bento with a simple and simply delicious citrus salad, you can rest assured that your kids are feeling the love.

DIY Hot Oatmeal with Apple + Dried Cranberries

½ cup old-fashioned oats

¼ cup chopped peeled apples

1 teaspoon brown sugar (or more to taste)

¼ teaspoon ground cinnamon

1¼ cups boiling water

1 tablespoon dried cranberries

1 tablespoon chopped pecans (optional)

1 tablespoon chopped walnuts (optional)

SERVES 1

STORAGE
5 hours in thermos

PREP TIME
5 minutes
COOK TIME
30 minutes in thermos

vegan

nut free

dairy free

gluten free

In a thermos, stir together the oats, apples, brown sugar, and cinnamon. Pour in the boiling water, stir, and cover with the thermos lid.

In a separate container, combine the dried cranberries with the pecans and walnuts (if using nuts).

The oatmeal will be ready in 30 minutes but will stay warm and ready to eat in the thermos for up to 5 hours. Stir in the cranberries and nuts (if using) just before eating.

INGREDIENT TIP: Some of my other favorite combos for add-ins are dried blueberries, flaxseed, and shredded coconut; chopped dried apricots and mango, cashew pieces, and chopped macadamia nuts; and chopped almonds, chia seeds, and raisins.

Spiced Carrot Muffins

MAKES
36 MINI OR
12 REGULAR-
SIZE MUFFINS

FREEZER
FRIENDLY

STORAGE
1 week in
airtight
container,
2 months in
freezer

PREP TIME
10 minutes
COOK TIME
20 minutes

veg

nut
free

1 cup white whole-wheat flour

½ cup whole-wheat flour

2 teaspoons baking powder

½ teaspoon baking soda

½ teaspoon salt

2 teaspoons ground cinnamon

½ teaspoon ground cloves

½ teaspoon ground allspice

½ cup applesauce

½ cup plain Greek yogurt, 2% or full-fat

½ cup extra-virgin olive oil, or butter or coconut oil, melted

2 large eggs

¼ cup brown sugar

1 teaspoon pure vanilla extract

1 cup finely grated carrots

⅓ cup chopped raisins (optional)

½ cup chopped walnuts (optional)

Preheat the oven to 375°F. Line 36 mini or 12 regular-size muffin cups with paper liners or generously coat with cooking spray and set aside.

In a large bowl, whisk together the flours, baking powder, baking soda, salt, cinnamon, cloves, and allspice.

In a medium bowl, whisk together the applesauce, yogurt, oil, eggs, brown sugar, vanilla extract, and raisins and walnuts (if using). Pour the wet ingredients into the dry ingredients and mix until just incorporated. Gently stir in the carrots. Fill the muffin cups two-thirds of the way full and bake for 18-20 minutes, or until golden brown.

Let cool completely.

BONUS RECIPE: I will totally high-five you if you make these muffins and then drizzle them with a cream cheese glaze. I am such a sucker for anything with cream cheese frosting. In a medium bowl, beat together ½ cup confectioners' sugar, 2 ounces cream cheese (at room temperature), ½ teaspoon pure vanilla extract, and 1 tablespoon milk, lemon juice, or orange juice until creamy, adding more milk or juice 1 teaspoon at a time, if needed, to thin out the glaze. Drizzle over the top of the muffins (put them on a paper towel or piece of parchment paper for easy cleanup) and enjoy.

Citrus Salad with Honey Dressing

1 tablespoon extra-virgin olive oil

1 tablespoon apple cider vinegar

1 teaspoon honey

1 blood orange, peeled and chopped

1 pink grapefruit, peeled and chopped

1 navel orange, peeled and chopped

In a small bowl, whisk together the olive oil, vinegar, and honey. Add the blood orange, grapefruit, and navel orange and gently mix until the citrus is coated.

MAKE IT A MEAL: One of my favorite ways to eat this salad for lunch is to start with a bed of fresh greens (kale, baby greens, spinach, Bibb, or a mixture), then add half of the dressed citrus salad, along with ¼ cup finely shredded fennel, ¼ cup diced avocado, 1 tablespoon chopped roasted almonds, and 1 serving of cooked chicken or salmon. Drizzle with a good-quality olive oil and serve.

SUBSTITUTION TIP: At certain times of year, it can be impossible to find blood oranges. If that's the case, you can sub fresh or canned pineapple chunks in their place.

SERVES 2

STORAGE
2 days in refrigerator

PREP TIME
5 minutes

veg

nut free

dairy free

gluten free

Breakfast for dinner = great idea. Breakfast for lunch = pure genius. Ellie goes crazy for any breakfast-for-lunch bento box combinations, and her box just about always comes home empty. These healthy little handheld quiches pack and transport well. The yogurt with homemade chia seed jam is beyond addicting and turns any plain yogurt into a delicious snack or main dish. Packed with some peas, grapes on a stick, and papayas dipped in spicy chocolate, this bento is a hit every time. A little savory + a little sweet = the perfect lunch combination.

Spinach + Cheese Quiches

Cooking spray

6 large eggs

½ cup milk

¾ cup shredded Cheddar cheese, divided

2 cups finely chopped fresh spinach

¼ cup plain bread crumbs (white, whole-wheat, or gluten-free)

Salt

Freshly ground black pepper

Preheat the oven to 350°F. Generously coat 24 mini or 10 regular-size muffin cups with cooking spray or line with paper liners, then coat with cooking spray.

In a medium bowl, whisk together the eggs and milk. Stir in ⅓ cup of cheese, the spinach, and the bread crumbs, then season with salt and pepper.

Sprinkle half of the remaining cheese equally in the bottom of each muffin cup, then pour the egg mixture into each cup two-thirds of the way full. Sprinkle the remaining cheese on top of each quiche and finally sprinkle just a pinch of freshly ground black pepper on top of each quiche.

Bake until the eggs are set, 15 to 20 minutes. Let cool for 10 minutes. Insert a small knife around the sides of each quiche to remove them from the pan. If you're freezing the quiches or adding them to a bento, let them cool completely first.

SUBSTITUTION TIP: Instead of using spinach, you can mix and match 2 cups of whatever veggies you have on hand—broccoli, leeks, kale, red or green bell peppers, or mushrooms. Just remember to chop the veggies into bite-site or smaller pieces, making it easier for your little one to eat them. You can also replace half of the veggies with cooked ground turkey or sausage for a little more protein if you wish. Have fun and mix it up each time you make this.

TIP: Silicon muffin liners work great for quiches! Not only do they make it easy to bake, since the quiches don't stick to them, the quiches are also super easy (and more durable) to transport.

Yogurt with Raspberry + Almond Chia Seed Jam

**MAKES
2 CUPS JAM**

STORAGE
jam only:
3 weeks in
refrigerator

PREP TIME
5 minutes
COOK TIME
15 minutes
COOL TIME
30 minutes

veg

gluten
free

2 cups frozen raspberries, thawed

1 cup frozen strawberries, thawed

3 tablespoons honey or maple syrup

2 tablespoons chia seeds

½ teaspoon pure almond extract

½ cup plain Greek yogurt, 2% or full-fat

In a medium pot, bring the raspberries and strawberries to a soft boil over medium heat. Reduce the heat to low and cook for 5 minutes, stirring often. Smash the berries with the back of a wooden spoon or potato masher for a chunkier jam; for a smoother jam, transfer the berries to a blender and purée for 30 seconds (then return the purée to the pot).

Stir in the honey and chia seeds and cook for 10 minutes more, stirring occasionally. Remove the pot from the heat, stir in the almond extract, and let cool for 30 minutes.

To pack for lunch, spoon the yogurt into a bento compartment and mix in 1 tablespoon of the jam.

INGREDIENT TIP: You can enjoy this easy jam with almost any dark berry or fruit (lighter fruits discolor when you add the chia seeds) such as blackberries, blueberries, strawberries, cranberries, and cherries. Some of my favorite combinations are cranberry + orange zest, blackberry + peach, and cherry + basil. The cooking method is the same for all the fruit, but the time you simmer the berries might be longer if the fruit is harder. Fresh or frozen both work great for this jam, so have fun and play around with whatever your family likes best or what's in season.

Dark Chocolate–Dipped Papayas

½ cup dark chocolate chips

Dash ground cinnamon

Dash ground nutmeg

Pinch cayenne pepper

3 cups dried papaya strips

MAKES
3 CUPS

STORAGE
2 weeks
in airtight
container

PREP TIME
5 minutes
COOL TIME
2 hours

veg

nut
free

gluten
free

Place a large sheet of parchment paper or a silicone mat on your work surface.

In a small microwave-safe bowl, heat the chocolate chips for 30-second intervals, stirring between each heating, until the chocolate is smooth and creamy, about 2 minutes total.

Stir in the cinnamon, nutmeg, and cayenne.

Dip each piece of papaya halfway into the melted chocolate, tapping on the side of the bowl to remove any excess chocolate. Lay each piece on the parchment paper.

Let cool until the chocolate is completely set, about 2 hours.

INGREDIENT TIP: This recipes works with any large pieces of dried fruit—apricot, pineapple, whole strawberries, and even prunes. I usually get an assortment of dried fruit and dip all at the same time so we have a variety of dried fruit treats for the week.

My family would eat pizza for every meal, every single day of the week—if I'd allow it. Without fail, Friday night is pizza and movie night at my house. I make a big family pizza along with an extra batch of dough, so later in the weekend I can make these healthier pizza rollups for upcoming lunches. Both the spinach pesto rollup featured in the bento and the alternative rollup recipe for veggies and pepperoni freeze and reheat well. They each include a big serving of veggies, so I don't feel at all bad about serving pizza to my family two (or three) times a week. The girls love dipping them in my simple pizza sauce. Packed in a bento with some fresh cut fruit and berries, it's a complete meal.

Spinach Pesto Pizza Rollups

Cooking spray

2 cups fresh spinach leaves

1 cup fresh basil leaves

Juice of 1 lemon

2 garlic cloves, peeled

1½ cups shredded Parmesan cheese, divided

Salt

Freshly ground black pepper

½ cup extra-virgin olive oil

1 recipe Whole-Wheat Pizza Dough (page 160) or store-bought pizza dough

2 cups shredded mozzarella cheese

Simple Pizza Sauce (page 58) or store-bought sauce, for dipping (optional)

MAKES
24 ROLLS

FREEZER
FRIENDLY

STORAGE
1 week in refrigerator, 2 months in freezer

PREP TIME
25 minutes
COOK TIME
20 minutes

veg

nut free

Preheat the oven to 400°F. Coat two baking sheets with cooking spray.

In a food processor or blender, combine the spinach, basil, lemon juice, garlic, ½ cup of Parmesan cheese, salt, and pepper, and blend until the spinach and basil are just chopped. With the machine running on high, slowly drizzle in the olive oil and blend for another minute, scraping down the sides of the bowl when needed.

On a lightly floured work surface, roll out the dough into a rectangle, roughly 18 by 9 inches. Evenly and lightly spread about half of the spinach pesto over the entire dough surface, leaving roughly 1 inch on the edge of the long sides clear of pesto but spreading all the way to the edge of the short sides. Sprinkle the mozzarella and another ½ cup of Parmesan over the pesto.

Start with the long side nearest you and tightly roll the dough away from you until you have a log shape. Gently roll the log back and forth to make sure the ingredients stay inside. Use your fingers to gently press the seam closed. Using a serrated knife, cut the roll into 1- to 2-inch-thick pieces. Place the rolls on the prepared baking sheets and sprinkle with the remaining ½ cup of Parmesan.

Bake until the crust is brown and the cheese is bubbly, about 20 minutes. Let cool for 5 minutes, then serve as is or with pizza sauce for dipping. If freezing or packing in a bento, let the rollups cool completely first.

INGREDIENT TIP: There will be about 1 cup of pesto leftover from this recipe. You can use it later in the week for a chicken spinach pasta dish or as a spread on your favorite grilled cheese sandwich, or freeze for the next time you make these rollups.

Simple Pizza Sauce

MAKES
4 CUPS

FREEZER
FRIENDLY

STORAGE
1 week in
refrigerator,
2 months in
freezer

PREP TIME
5 minutes
COOK TIME
10 minutes

veg

nut
free

dairy
free

gluten
free

1 (28-ounce) can whole
tomatoes, drained

4 garlic cloves, peeled

2 tablespoons extra-virgin olive oil

2 teaspoons balsamic vinegar

1 teaspoon honey

1 teaspoon salt

½ teaspoon freshly ground
black pepper

½ teaspoon dried oregano

¼ teaspoon dried thyme

⅛ teaspoon red pepper flakes

Combine the tomatoes, garlic, olive oil, vinegar, honey, salt, and pepper in a blender or food processor and blend for 1 minute, scraping down the sides of the bowl as needed. Stir or gently pulse in the oregano, thyme, and red pepper flakes.

This sauce can be used right away on a pizza. For a thicker and deeper-flavored sauce (perfect for pasta night), transfer the purée to a medium saucepan and bring to a boil over high heat. Then reduce the heat to low and simmer, covered, for 10 to 15 minutes.

INGREDIENT TIP: If tomatoes are in season, you can use 2 pounds quartered ripe tomatoes in this recipe. You will need to adjust the seasoning to accommodate their fresh taste. I also find that roasting the tomatoes at 450°F for 30 minutes really boosts their natural flavors.

Veggie-Loaded Pepperoni Pizza Rollups

Cooking spray

1 tablespoon extra-virgin olive oil

½ cup chopped carrot

½ cup chopped red bell pepper

½ cup chopped orange bell pepper

¼ cup chopped broccoli

¼ cup chopped spinach leaves

1½ cups Simple Pizza Sauce (page 58) or store-bought sauce, plus additional for dipping

2 tablespoons tomato paste

Salt

Freshly ground black pepper

1 recipe Whole-Wheat Pizza Dough (page 160) or store-bought pizza dough

2 cups shredded mozzarella cheese

5 ounces pepperoni, sliced

MAKES 24 ROLLS

FREEZER FRIENDLY

STORAGE
1 week in refrigerator, 2 months in freezer

PREP TIME
25 minutes
COOK TIME
20 minutes

nut free

Preheat the oven to 400°F. Spray two baking sheets with cooking spray and set aside.

In a medium skillet, heat the olive oil over medium heat. Add the carrot, red pepper, orange pepper, broccoli, and spinach and cook, stirring frequently, until the carrots are tender, 5 to 7 minutes.

Transfer the vegetables to a blender or food processor and add the pizza sauce, tomato paste, salt, and pepper. Blend on high, scraping down the sides of the bowl if needed, until the sauce is only slightly chunky, about 1 minute.

On a lightly floured work surface, roll out the dough into a rectangle, roughly 18 by 9 inches. Evenly and lightly spread about half of the veggie sauce over the entire dough surface, leaving roughly 1 inch on the edge of the long sides clear of sauce but spreading all the way to the edge of the short sides. Sprinkle the mozzarella over the sauce and layer the pepperoni slices over the cheese.

Start with the long side nearest you and tightly roll the dough away from you until you have a log shape. Gently roll the log back and forth to make sure the ingredients stay inside. Use your fingers to gently press the seam closed. Using a serrated knife, cut the roll into 1- to 2-inch-thick pieces. Place the rolls on the prepared baking sheets.

Bake until the crust is brown and the cheese is bubbly, about 20 minutes. Let cool for 5 minutes, then serve as is or with pizza sauce for dipping. If freezing or packing in a bento, let the rollups cool completely first.

Take the basic grilled cheese up a notch! I love using sharp Cheddar and tart Granny Smith apples paired with tangy Dijon mustard and sweet jam in this recipe. Made in just around 10 minutes, this sandwich makes for a great quick lunch or easy dinner when you are short on time. Serve with rainbow carrot sticks for a well-balanced and colorful meal.

Grilled Cheese + Apple Sandwich

4 slices bread

1 tablespoon unsalted butter at room temperature

2 teaspoons Dijon mustard

2 teaspoons cherry or raspberry jam

½ cup shredded sharp Cheddar cheese

1 apple, cored and thinly sliced

SERVES 2

PREP TIME
5 minutes
COOK TIME
6 minutes

veg

nut free

Lay out the four slices of bread. Lightly butter one side of each piece of bread, then flip them over. On two slices, spread the Dijon mustard. On the two remaining slices, spread the jam.

Top the Dijon side of one bread slice with a sprinkling of the cheese, then lay 3 apple slices over it. Sprinkle on another layer of cheese and top with the bread slice with jam. The jam side should touch the cheese. Repeat with the remaining two bread slices and ingredients.

In a medium skillet, grill the sandwiches over medium heat until golden brown, about 3 minutes. Flip and grill for another 3 minutes. Cut each sandwich on the diagonal. Serve warm or let cool completely before adding to the bento.

INGREDIENT TIP: If you have the time (and ingredients), it's easy to kick this sandwich up about 10 notches of yumminess. Add 2 slices of cooked bacon and 2 slices of sliced deli turkey on top of the apples and cook according to the directions, lightly pressing on the sandwich with a spatula while it cooks to make all of the layers stick together.

3

Winter

It can be hard in the cold and hectic winter months to spend time making healthy lunches when you are just trying your best to keep the mound of boots, hats, mittens, scarves, and puffy winter coats in check as your kids come barreling into the house. The following recipes are a collection of my family's favorite warm, quick, and healthy meals. I tend to make these over and over again. Some of them we have for dinner and then I pack the leftovers, while others I put together quickly before the morning winter gear battle begins.

Bring a little game day fare into your kids' winter bento box with a fun 5-layer bean dip, spiced baked tortilla dippers, tricolor pepper dippers, and black olives. And don't forget the post-game celebration—dessert. White chocolate–covered pretzels with pistachio sprinkles, to be specific, because every meal needs a touch of fancy. This crowd-favorite bean dip is given a healthy twist by using homemade "refried" beans, a Greek yogurt and lime sauce in place of sour cream, and a big batch of baked spiced tortilla dippers with salsa. Healthy food that pleases the entire family. Touchdown!

5-Layer Bean Dip

FOR THE BEAN LAYER

2 (15-ounce) cans black beans, rinsed and drained

Juice of 1 lime

1½ teaspoons ground cumin

1 teaspoon garlic powder

1 teaspoon salt

½ teaspoon freshly ground black pepper

⅛ teaspoon cayenne pepper

FOR THE AVOCADO LAYER

1 ripe avocado, pitted, peeled, and diced

Juice of 1 lime

½ teaspoon garlic powder

Salt

Freshly ground black pepper

Pinch cayenne pepper (optional)

FOR THE CREAM LAYER

½ cup plain Greek yogurt, 2% or full-fat

Juice of ½ lime

FOR THE TOPPINGS

½ cup shredded Cheddar cheese

½ cup chopped tomatoes

SERVES 4 TO 6

STORAGE
4 days in refrigerator (bean and cream layers), 1 day in refrigerator (avocado layer)

PREP TIME
20 minutes
COOK TIME
10 minutes

veg

nut free

gluten free

To make the bean layer, combine all the ingredients in a blender or food processor and pulse in 5-second increments until smooth, about 30 seconds total. Scrape down the sides of the bowl between pulses, if needed.

Transfer the beans to a medium saucepan and heat over medium heat until the beans are warm, about 10 minutes.

Meanwhile, in a small bowl, make the avocado layer by smashing the diced avocado until creamy but still chunky. Stir in the lime juice, garlic powder, salt, black pepper, and cayenne pepper (if using).

In another small bowl, make the cream layer by mixing the Greek yogurt and lime juice.

In a bowl or bento box compartment, assemble the dip by layering ½ cup beans, 2 tablespoons cream sauce, and 2 tablespoons avocado. If packing for lunch, let the beans cool completely. Sprinkle with 1 tablespoon shredded Cheddar cheese and top it off with 1 tablespoon chopped tomatoes. Serve or refrigerate right away.

Baked Spiced Tortilla Dippers

SERVES 4

STORAGE
2 days in
partially open
container

PREP TIME
5 minutes
COOK TIME
8 to 10 minutes

vegan

nut
free

dairy
free

gluten
free

Cooking spray

8 medium corn, whole-wheat, or white flour tortillas

2 to 3 tablespoons extra-virgin olive oil, for brushing

1 teaspoon chili powder

1 teaspoon garlic powder

1 teaspoon salt

Preheat the oven to 400°F. Lightly spray a baking sheet with cooking spray and set aside.

Brush one tortilla with olive oil, flip it over, and brush the other side with more oil. Stack another tortilla on top of the first and brush it with olive oil. The oil from the first tortilla will rub onto the bottom of the second tortilla. Continue to stack and brush the tortillas with olive oil until all are coated.

Divide the stack in half (2 stacks of 4 tortillas). Cut each stack down the middle and then into either 1-inch strips or traditional wedge shapes.

Spread out the tortilla strips or wedges in an even layer on the baking sheet. Sprinkle them with the chili powder, garlic powder, and salt.

For corn tortillas, bake until just golden brown, 8 to 10 minutes. For flour tortillas, bake for 8 minutes, flip them, and then bake until golden brown, another 6 to 8 minutes. Let the chips cool on the baking sheet. They will get crispier as they cool.

BONUS RECIPE: I highly recommend doubling the number of tortillas used in the recipe but making half of the chips into cinnamon-sugar tortilla dippers. These sweet chips are perfect to dip into vanilla yogurt, crumble on top of vanilla bean ice cream, or eat straight out of the pan while no one is looking. (My opinion is that flour tortillas are best for this, but corn tortillas also work for the gluten-free crowd.) Follow the recipe through step 3. Then, in a small bowl, combine 3 tablespoons sugar with 1 teaspoon ground cinnamon. Sprinkle the cinnamon sugar generously over the cut tortillas and bake according to the directions. Some of the sugar may stick to the baking sheet, so line the baking sheet with parchment paper or a silicone mat and let the baked dippers cool on a cutting board or wire rack.

White Chocolate + Pistachio Pretzels

½ cup white chocolate chips

3 cups pretzels, rods or twists

2 tablespoons finely chopped pistachios

MAKES
3 CUPS

STORAGE
1 week in
airtight
container

PREP TIME
15 minutes
COOL TIME
1 hour

veg

In a small microwave-safe bowl, heat the white chocolate chips in the microwave in 30-second intervals, stirring after each interval, until the chocolate has melted, about 2 minutes total.

Place a sheet of parchment paper or a silicone mat on the counter.

Dip each pretzel halfway into the chocolate, gently tapping the side of the bowl to remove any excess chocolate. You can dip the pretzel all the way, but you will need to increase the amount of chocolate chips to 1 cup. Lay each pretzel on the parchment paper. Continue this process until you have roughly 8 to 10 pretzels completed. Then sprinkle the chocolate with the chopped pistachios. Repeat this step until all the pretzels are used.

Let cool on the counter for 1 hour and then store in an airtight container.

SUBSTITUTION TIP: If you want to go nut-free, s-p-r-i-n-k-l-e-s (must spell out that word in my house) are a great way to add a little colorful fun to your kid's bento box.

The first time I sent dark chocolate haystacks to school with Ellie, she came home with chocolate smeared all over her belly. *Under her shirt.* I couldn't understand how even my messy child could do this. When I asked her teacher the next morning what happened, it turns out the kids sitting at her table were trying to get their hands on them, so she decided to hide them—under her shirt! The chocolate haystacks are a nice end (or more likely beginning) to a satisfying lunch of coconut rice with snap peas and edamame (or an easy veggie and pineapple rice as an alternative). These Asia-inspired rice dishes are full of protein and fiber as well as colorful vegetables that hopefully even the pickiest of eaters will devour. Add some sliced strawberries and pomegranate seeds for a perfect balance to the chocolate for dessert.

Coconut Rice with Snap Peas + Edamame

2 tablespoons coconut oil, extra-virgin olive oil, or unsalted butter

½ cup snap peas, roughly chopped

½ cup frozen edamame, thawed

2 cups cooked brown or white rice

1 teaspoon grated fresh ginger or ½ teaspoon ground ginger

½ teaspoon ground cumin

½ teaspoon salt

⅓ cup unsweetened shredded coconut, toasted

SERVES 4

FREEZER FRIENDLY

STORAGE
1 week in refrigerator, 2 months in freezer

PREP TIME
5 minutes
COOK TIME
6 minutes

vegan

nut free

dairy free

gluten free

In a large skillet, heat the oil over medium heat. Add the snap peas and edamame and cook for 3 minutes, stirring frequently. Add the cooked rice, ginger, cumin, and salt, and mix well. Cook for another 3 minutes, stirring frequently.

Remove the pan from the heat and add the toasted coconut. Stir well and serve. If packing in a bento, it should be at room temperature or served warm in a thermos.

SUBSTITUTION TIP: For an even more intense coconut flavor, when cooking the rice, replace half of the cooking water with canned coconut milk.

Dark Chocolate Haystacks

Cooking spray

1 cup dark chocolate chips

¾ cup dried cranberries

¾ cup sliced almonds

2 cups broken thin pretzel sticks

½ teaspoon coarse sea salt (optional)

Lightly spray a baking sheet with cooking spray or line it with parchment paper or a silicone mat.

In a medium microwave-safe bowl, heat the chocolate chips in the microwave in 30-second intervals, stirring after each interval, until the chocolate is melted and smooth. Add the cranberries, sliced almonds, and pretzel sticks and stir until everything is evenly coated.

Using two spoons, scoop up roughly a tablespoon of the mixture and drop the "haystack" onto the baking sheet. The mixture is crumbly, so make sure all the pieces are lightly packed and touching. As the chocolate hardens, the haystacks will stick together.

Lightly sprinkle the haystacks with sea salt (if using) and let cool until the chocolate has set, about 2 hours.

INGREDIENT TIP: You can use almost any dried fruit or nuts/seeds in this recipe. Any combination of dried cherries, dried blueberries, raisins, golden raisins, dried strawberries, roasted pumpkin seeds, roasted sesame seeds, peanuts, pistachios, and mini marshmallows all work. Just keep the add-ins to no more than a total of 1½ cups and you are sure to have a winning combination. For a delicious nut-free option, use ¾ cup roughly chopped dried cherries, ½ cup pepitas (toasted pumpkin seeds), and ½ cup toasted sesame seeds.

Easy Veggie + Pineapple Rice

2 tablespoons tamari or reduced-sodium soy sauce

1 tablespoon toasted sesame oil

2 garlic cloves, minced

1 teaspoon grated fresh ginger or ½ teaspoon ground ginger

2 tablespoons coconut oil, extra-virgin olive oil, or unsalted butter

½ red bell pepper, finely chopped

1 carrot, finely chopped

½ cup peas, thawed if frozen

2 cups cooked white or brown rice

1 cup diced pineapple, fresh or canned and drained

2 scallions, sliced

SERVES 4

FREEZER FRIENDLY

STORAGE
1 week in refrigerator, 2 months in freezer

PREP TIME
15 minutes
COOK TIME
10 minutes

vegan

nut free

dairy free

gluten free

In a small bowl, whisk together the tamari, sesame oil, garlic, and ginger.

In a large skillet, heat the oil over medium heat. Add the red pepper and carrot and cook for 5 minutes, stirring frequently. Add the peas and cook for another 3 minutes, stirring frequently. Add the rice, pineapple, scallions, and tamari mixture and cook until everything is heated through, about 2 minutes. If packing in a bento, let cool to room temperature or serve warm in a thermos.

MAKE IT A MEAL: I love adding cooked chicken or pork to this rice for more protein. Before sautéing the vegetables, heat an additional 1 tablespoon of coconut oil, extra-virgin olive oil, or unsalted butter in a large skillet. Sauté 8 ounces of chopped cooked meat until cooked through, 7 to 10 minutes. Transfer the meat to a plate and set aside. Continue cooking by sautéing the remaining ingredients in the skillet, as instructed. Before serving, toss in the cooked meat, heat through, and serve.

During the cold months, all you really need is a warm, comforting chili, some kickin' corn muffins, and a good hot toddy. These are my family's favorites (the first two, that is) and while I usually let a big pot of this kid-friendly chili simmer on my stove all afternoon, it can be made in less than 30 minutes for a fast weeknight meal. But let's talk about how I put a big ol' serving of chopped broccoli into my corn muffins and my girls don't even blink an eye at those little speckles of green. I also add Cheddar cheese, so I guess it all balances out. The lunch bento rounds out with some cocoa + cinnamon nuts and a handful of grapes.

Kid-Friendly Veggie Chili

1 tablespoon extra-virgin olive oil

½ onion, finely chopped

2 garlic cloves, minced

1 large carrot, finely chopped

½ red bell pepper, chopped

1 (15-ounce) can pinto beans, rinsed and drained

1 (15-ounce) can kidney beans, rinsed and drained

1 (15-ounce) can black beans, rinsed and drained

1 (14-ounce) can diced tomatoes, undrained

1 (14-ounce) can tomato sauce

1 (14-ounce) can vegetable or chicken broth, plus additional if needed

1 cup corn, fresh or frozen (no need to thaw)

2 tablespoons chili powder

1 tablespoon dried cilantro

1 tablespoon ground cumin

1 teaspoon paprika

1 teaspoon salt

½ teaspoon freshly ground black pepper

SERVES 8

FREEZER FRIENDLY

STORAGE
1 week in refrigerator, 2 months in freezer

PREP TIME
15 minutes
COOK TIME
20 minutes

vegan

nut free

dairy free

gluten free

In a large stockpot, heat the oil over medium-high heat. Add the onion and cook until softened, about 3 minutes. Add the garlic and cook, stirring occasionally, for 1 minute. Add the carrot and red pepper, and cook for 5 minutes.

Add the pinto beans, kidney beans, black beans, diced tomatoes and their juice, tomato sauce, broth, corn, chili powder, cilantro, cumin, paprika, salt, and black pepper, and bring everything to a boil. Reduce the heat to a simmer and cook for at least 10 minutes, but you can let it simmer for as long as you want. If the chili gets too thick, add an additional cup or two of broth or water.

Let cool slightly and serve. If packing for lunch, it will stay warm in a thermos for up to 5 hours.

PREP TIP: If your little one is in a no-veggie phase, you can blend the vegetables to "hide" them. While this isn't my favorite approach, at some point it's nice to have one meal where you're not saying, "Eat your veggies." Combine the cooked carrot, red pepper, diced tomatoes, and tomato sauce in a blender or food processor and blend until smooth, about 1 minute. Return the purée to the chili and cook as instructed in step 2.

Broccoli + Cheddar Corn Muffins

MAKES
36 MINI OR
12 REGULAR-
SIZE MUFFINS

FREEZER
FRIENDLY

STORAGE
1 week in
airtight
container,
2 months in
freezer

PREP TIME
10 minutes
COOK TIME
10 to
15 minutes

veg

nut
free

1¼ cups white whole-wheat, whole-wheat, or all-purpose flour

¾ cup yellow cornmeal

¼ cup sugar

2 teaspoons baking powder

½ teaspoon salt

1 cup milk

2 large eggs

⅓ cup extra-virgin olive oil or melted coconut oil

¼ cup honey

½ cup shredded sharp Cheddar cheese

1 cup corn, fresh or frozen and thawed

1 cup finely chopped broccoli

Preheat the oven to 350°F. Line 36 mini or 12 regular-size muffin cups with paper liners. These muffins will definitely stick if you don't use the liners!

In a large bowl, whisk together the flour, cornmeal, sugar, baking powder, and salt.

Gently stir in the milk, eggs, oil, and honey just until incorporated.

Gently fold in the cheese, corn, and broccoli just until incorporated. The mixture will be slightly lumpy and thick.

Fill each muffin cup three-quarters of the way full. Bake until golden brown on top, 10 to 12 minutes for mini muffins or 15 to 18 minutes for regular-size muffins. Let cool for 10 minutes before serving. If packing in a bento, let the muffins cool completely.

PREP TIP: If you are short on time, you can use a box of corn muffin mix to start this recipe—just make sure the mix makes 12 muffins. Mix the corn muffin batter as directed on the box, then stir in the cheese, corn, and broccoli at the very end.

Cocoa + Cinnamon Spiced Nuts

Cooking spray

2 tablespoons sugar

2 tablespoons unsweetened cocoa powder

1 teaspoon ground cinnamon

½ teaspoon ground ginger

½ teaspoon salt

1 large egg white

3 cups nuts (such as cashews, almonds, and peanuts)

MAKES 3 CUPS

STORAGE
2 weeks
in airtight
container

PREP TIME
10 minutes
COOK TIME
20 minutes

veg

dairy free

gluten free

Preheat the oven to 300°F. Spray a baking sheet with cooking spray, or line it with a silicone mat, and set aside.

In a small bowl, stir together the sugar, cocoa, cinnamon, ginger, and salt.

In a medium bowl, whisk the egg white. Mix in the nuts until well coated. Pour in the spice mixture and mix until well coated.

Pour the nuts in an even layer onto the baking sheet and bake for 20 minutes, stirring them at the 10-minute mark. Cool completely.

BONUS RECIPE: For a more savory spiced nut, mix 2 tablespoons brown sugar, 1 teaspoon mild curry powder, ½ teaspoon ground cumin, and ¼ teaspoon salt for the spice mixture. These savory nuts are especially good chopped and used in a salad of dark leafy greens, slices of warm grilled chicken, chunks of feta, sliced strawberries, diced cucumbers (or zucchini), and all drizzled with Basic Vinaigrette (page 163). For kids, serve this as a deconstructed salad with no lettuce and the vinaigrette as a dipping sauce.

This is my ode to my favorite school lunch when I was a kid—PB&J. I've updated it with seed butter, so it's completely nut-free, and present it on a stick. If you're too nervous to send your kid to school with a stick in her lunch, simply forgo it. To Ellie's bento box I add the most addicting sweet Cajun party mix that could ever be made. I finish off the lunch with mini whole-wheat chocolate chip cookies and a quick green salad of diced apple and kiwi fruit with a few frozen peas. The best part is you get to sit back at the end of the day and eat the remaining 11 cups of party mix!

Seed Butter + Jelly Sandwich on a Stick

2 cups sunflower seeds, raw or unsalted toasted

3 tablespoons coconut oil

1 tablespoon pure maple syrup

1 teaspoon ground cinnamon

¼ teaspoon ground nutmeg

⅛ teaspoon sea salt

4 slices bread (whole-wheat, white, or gluten-free)

1 tablespoon favorite jam or jelly

10 blackberries or strawberries

**MAKES
1½ CUPS
SEED BUTTER**

STORAGE
(seed butter only): 3 weeks in airtight container or refrigerator

PREP TIME
15 minutes
COOK TIME
5 minutes

vegan

nut free

dairy free

gluten free

In a medium skillet, toast the sunflower seeds over medium heat, stirring frequently, until golden brown, 5 to 10 minutes. Transfer to a paper towel and let cool slightly.

In a food processor or blender, blend the seeds, scraping down the sides of the bowl if needed, until the seeds look like sand, about 2 minutes. Add the coconut oil, maple syrup, cinnamon, nutmeg, and sea salt and blend for 5 to 7 minutes, scraping down the sides if needed. Be patient. At first it will look like this isn't going to work. But keep blending, as it takes at least 5 minutes to see the sesame seeds turning into seed butter. As soon as it begins to look like seed butter, run the blender for an additional 1 to 2 minutes to get it really smooth. The total run time will be about 10 minutes.

Make the sandwiches by gently flattening out the bread slices with a rolling pin or large jar. For the best results, the bread should be roughly ¼ inch thick. Divide 1 tablespoon seed butter between two bread slices and spread across each slice. Divide the jam across the other two bread slices and spread across each slice. Place the jam slices jam-side down over the seed butter slices.

Press a small round cookie cutter or jar into the bread all the way through, cutting around the cutter with a knife if needed. Cut out as many rounds as you can. Slide two sandwich rounds onto a skewer, followed by a blackberry, another two sandwich rounds, and a second blackberry. Or you can use any skewer configuration you want. Repeat until all the sandwich rounds and blackberries are used. You'll likely have 4 to 6 skewers depending on the size of the sandwich rounds. (Of course you can also just cut each sandwich into triangles and serve with the blackberries on the side.)

Sweet Cajun Party Mix

Cooking spray

9 cups mixed cereal (wheat, corn, or rice Chex, Cheerios, bran flakes, etc.)

1 cup mini pretzel twists

1 cup cashews (optional)

1 cup cheese crackers, such as Cheddar Bunnies

6 tablespoons unsalted butter or coconut oil

2 tablespoons Worcestershire sauce

2 tablespoons honey

2 teaspoons Cajun spice mix

1 teaspoon garlic powder

½ teaspoon salt

Preheat the oven to 250°F. Lightly coat two baking sheets with cooking spray.

In a large bowl, combine the cereal, pretzels, cashews (if using), and cheese crackers.

In a small microwave-safe bowl, heat the butter, Worcestershire sauce, honey, Cajun spice, garlic powder, and salt in 15-second intervals, stirring after each interval, until the butter is melted, about 45 seconds. Pour the butter mixture over the cereal and mix until everything is evenly coated.

Spread out the cereal mixture in an even layer on the prepared baking sheets and bake for 1 hour, stirring the cereal and rotating the trays every 15 minutes. Let cool completely.

INGREDIENT TIP: I love adding air-popped popcorn to this party mix. As soon as the cereal comes out of the oven, stir 3 cups of air-popped popcorn into the mix and let it cool completely.

BONUS RECIPE: If you can't find Cajun spice mix, it's easy to make your own. In a small bowl, mix 2½ teaspoons paprika, 2 teaspoons garlic powder, 2 teaspoons salt, 1 teaspoon freshly ground black pepper, 1 teaspoon onion powder, 1 teaspoon dried oregano, 1 teaspoon dried thyme, and ½ teaspoon cayenne pepper. Store in an airtight container. It's great on grilled chicken, oven-roasted potatoes, burgers, or even your favorite sloppy Joe recipe.

Whole-Wheat Chocolate Chip Cookies

½ cup whole-wheat flour

½ cup white whole-wheat flour

½ teaspoon baking powder

½ teaspoon baking soda

½ teaspoon salt

½ cup unsalted butter or coconut oil, at room temperature

⅓ cup granulated sugar

¼ cup brown sugar

1 large egg

½ teaspoon pure vanilla extract

1 cup chocolate chips or mini chocolate chips

MAKES 36 MINI COOKIES OR 18 REGULAR-SIZE

FREEZER FRIENDLY

STORAGE
1 week in airtight container, 2 months in freezer

PREP TIME
10 minutes
COOK TIME
10 minutes

veg

nut free

Preheat the oven to 350°F. Line two baking sheets with parchment paper or silicone mats.

In a medium bowl, whisk together the flours, baking powder, baking soda, and salt.

In another medium bowl or the bowl of a stand mixer, beat together the butter and sugars until smooth. Add the egg and the vanilla extract and beat until combined, scraping down the sides of the bowl if needed. With the mixer on low speed, add the flour mixture and mix until just combined. Use a spatula to gently fold in the chocolate chips.

For mini cookies, drop or roll the dough onto the baking sheets in 1-teaspoon mounds. For regular-size cookies, drop or roll the dough onto the baking sheets in 1-tablespoon mounds.

Bake until golden brown, 9 to 11 minutes. Let cool for 2 minutes on the baking sheets, then transfer to a wire rack to cool completely.

PREP TIP: Because I will eat the entire batch of these cookies in two days—no willpower here—I like to roll half of the dough into 1-tablespoon balls and freeze them. Then when the girls deserve a special treat, I pop a few onto a baking sheet and bake as directed. Of course I bake one or two for myself. Parents deserve a special treat, too.

On the morning of the season's first snow, I wake the girls early and we all bundle up (me in five extra layers, the girls in practically nothing) and huddle together under blankets on our favorite bench watching the falling snow. Cinnamon crackers and mugs of hot chocolate are our go-to treats. They're synonymous with winter, even if only at my house. For an all-around flavorful and filling lunch, my classic Italian meatballs are protein-packed, delicious, and easy to eat. If you have a child who loves well-spiced foods, opt for the alternative Vietnamese meatball recipe. This bento is rounded out by cut peppers with ranch dip, fresh blackberries, and pomegranate seeds.

Italian Turkey Meatballs

Cooking spray

1 pound lean ground turkey

½ cup panko bread crumbs

1 large egg, lightly beaten

1 tablespoon dried Italian seasoning blend

1 teaspoon garlic powder

1 teaspoon sea salt

MAKES
24 MEATBALLS
(6 SERVINGS)

FREEZER
FRIENDLY

STORAGE
4 days in
refrigerator,
2 months in
freezer

PREP TIME
5 minutes
COOK TIME
20 minutes

nut
free

dairy
free

Preheat the oven to 400°F. Lightly coat a baking sheet with cooking spray or line it with a silicone mat, and set aside.

In a medium bowl, combine all the ingredients and gently mix with a wooden spoon or your hands. Lightly shape the meat mixture into 1½-inch balls. Place the meatballs on the prepared baking sheet and bake for 20 minutes, gently flipping halfway through the baking time.

Let the meatballs cool slightly before serving. If packing for lunch, cool completely before adding to the bento box or serve warm in a thermos.

INGREDIENT TIP: I love adding extra veggies to my meatballs, but the trick is to make sure they are not wet, as that will make the meatballs fall apart. So, carrots, zucchini, beets, and squash should be grated and then rolled in a paper towel to squeeze out any excess water. Frozen spinach or kale should be thawed and blotted as well. For this recipe, I often add ½ cup finely chopped fresh spinach and ¼ cup shredded zucchini for some extra nutritional value.

Super Cinnamon Crackers

**MAKES
3 CUPS**

**FREEZER
FRIENDLY**

STORAGE
1 week in
airtight
container,
2 months in
freezer

PREP TIME
5 minutes
CHILL TIME
2 to 12 hours
COOK TIME
10 minutes

veg

nut
free

¾ cup all-purpose or white whole-wheat flour, plus additional for dusting

½ cup brown sugar

2 tablespoons ground cinnamon

¼ teaspoon baking powder

¼ teaspoon salt

⅓ cup cold unsalted butter, cut into pieces

3 tablespoons milk

Cooking spray

2 tablespoons granulated sugar, for sprinkling

Combine the flour, brown sugar, cinnamon, baking powder, salt, and butter in a food processor and pulse until the ingredients turn into a coarse crumble. Add the milk and continue to pulse until a dough ball forms. Remove the dough from the food processor, flatten it into a disk, and cover it with plastic wrap. Chill in the refrigerator for at least 2 hours or up to overnight.

When ready to bake, preheat the oven to 350°F. Take the dough out of the refrigerator and let it sit on the counter for 20 minutes. Lightly coat a baking sheet with cooking spray or line it with parchment paper or a silicone mat.

On a lightly floured surface, roll out the dough to ⅛-inch thickness. Cut it by using small cookie cutters or making squares or triangles with a knife. Place the cut dough on the baking sheet. The crackers will spread only a little bit, so you can lay them out almost touching. Sprinkle with the granulated sugar.

Bake until golden brown, 10 to 12 minutes. Let the crackers cool for 2 minutes on the baking sheet and then transfer them to a wire rack to cool completely.

BONUS RECIPE: Prefer a savory cracker to a sweet one? In my cookbook *Little Foodie*, I include a recipe for Cheddar and rosemary crackers that the kids (and I) love. To make them, prepare the dough with 6 ounces shredded white Cheddar cheese, ¼ cup cubed unsalted butter, ¾ cup whole-wheat flour, 1 teaspoon salt, ½ teaspoon garlic powder, and 1 teaspoon finely chopped fresh rosemary. Follow the same steps, but skip the sprinkling of sugar in step 3.

Vietnamese Meatballs

FOR THE DIPPING SAUCE

3 tablespoons canned coconut milk

1 tablespoon tamari or reduced-sodium soy sauce

1 tablespoon rice wine vinegar

1 teaspoon Thai red curry paste

1 teaspoon honey

Juice of ½ lime

Sriracha (optional)

FOR THE MEATBALLS

1 pound lean ground chicken, turkey, or beef

½ cup panko bread crumbs

⅓ cup finely chopped onion

2 garlic cloves, minced

1 tablespoon grated fresh ginger

⅓ cup finely chopped fresh cilantro

1 tablespoon finely chopped fresh mint

2 tablespoons tamari or reduced-sodium soy sauce

1 teaspoon sea salt

½ teaspoon freshly ground black pepper

2 tablespoons extra-virgin olive oil

MAKES 24 MEATBALLS (SERVES 6)

FREEZER FRIENDLY

STORAGE
4 days in refrigerator, 2 months in freezer

PREP TIME
10 minutes
COOK TIME
10 minutes

nut free

In a small bowl, stir together all the dipping sauce ingredients until well combined. Set aside.

In a medium bowl, mix the ground meat, bread crumbs, onion, garlic, ginger, cilantro, mint, tamari, sea salt, and pepper gently with a wooden spoon or your hands. Gently shape the meat mixture into 1½-tablespoon balls.

Heat the olive oil in a large skillet over medium-high heat. Working in batches, add the meatballs and cook for 5 minutes. Flip the meatballs over, cover, and cook until the meatballs are golden brown and cooked all the way through, about 5 minutes more. Serve warm in a thermos or cool completely before packing in a bento, and pack the dipping sauce separately.

BENTO

14

While my girls are not old enough to pack their own lunches yet, I let them have choices as often as possible. The garlic noodles recipe is great for allowing your children to pick what they want as add-ins. But don't limit yourself to the options I give you; almost anything in your fridge will work with these simple (but tasty) noodles—see the tip at the end of the recipe for more suggestions. Complete the bento with a scrumptious raspberry and orange oat square, along with a berry skewer and kiwi fruit halves.

DIY Garlic Noodles with Chicken, Bacon, Peas + Cheese

1 (16-ounce) package of spaghetti (whole-wheat, regular, or gluten-free)

¼ cup tamari or reduced-sodium soy sauce

¼ cup water

2 tablespoons brown sugar

2 tablespoons grated fresh ginger

4 garlic cloves, minced

2 teaspoons toasted sesame oil

2 scallions, sliced, for garnish (optional)

SUGGESTED ADD-INS, PER SERVING

¼ cup cubed cooked chicken

1 tablespoon fresh peas, or frozen and thawed

1 slice crisp cooked bacon

1 heaping tablespoon white Cheddar cheese

SERVES 8

STORAGE
4 days in refrigerator

PREP TIME
5 minutes
COOK TIME
10 minutes

nut free

gluten free

Bring a large pot of salted water to a boil over high heat and cook the pasta according to the package directions until al dente.

Meanwhile, in a small bowl, whisk together the tamari, water, brown sugar, ginger, garlic, and sesame oil.

When the pasta is done, drain and return it to the pot. Add the sauce and toss until the pasta is completely coated. Stir in the desired add-ins, and garnish with the sliced scallions (if using). Serve hot or cold. If packing in a bento, the noodles should be at room temperature, and the add-ins should be packed separately.

SUBSTITUTION TIP: In addition to or instead of the chicken, peas, bacon, and cheese, you might want to offer steamed broccoli, small slices of grilled steak, stir-fried peppers, corn, sliced cucumbers, crispy tofu cubes, shredded carrots, chunks of feta, chopped peanuts, or halved cherry tomatoes. While we enjoy this dish cold for lunch, you can easily send the noodles warm in a thermos, with the add-ins in a separate bento container.

Raspberry + Orange Oat Bars

MAKES 16
(2-INCH)
BARS

FREEZER
FRIENDLY

STORAGE
1 week in
airtight
container,
2 months in
freezer

PREP TIME
15 minutes
COOK TIME
30 minutes
COOL TIME
2 hours

veg

nut
free

½ cup unsalted butter, melted

¼ cup packed brown sugar, plus 1 tablespoon

¼ cup granulated sugar

½ teaspoon pure vanilla extract

1 cup old-fashioned oats

1 cup white whole-wheat flour

¼ teaspoon baking soda

¼ teaspoon salt

¼ teaspoon ground nutmeg

¾ cup seedless raspberry jam

1 teaspoon grated orange zest

Preheat the oven to 350°F. Line an 8-inch square baking pan with parchment paper.

In a medium bowl, stir together the melted butter, ¼ cup of brown sugar, granulated sugar, and vanilla extract. Add the oats, flour, baking soda, salt, and nutmeg and stir to combine. The mixture will be lumpy and a little crumbly. Set aside 1 cup of the crumb mixture. Transfer the remaining mixture to the prepared pan and press down firmly with your fingers or the back of a wooden spoon until the crust is flat, even, and smooth.

In a small bowl, stir together the raspberry jam and orange zest. Evenly spread the raspberry mixture over the crust in the pan.

Pour the reserved crumb mixture back into the medium bowl and mix in the remaining 1 tablespoon of brown sugar. Evenly sprinkle this on top of the raspberry jam.

Bake until golden brown, about 30 minutes. Place the pan on a wire rack and let cool for 2 hours before slicing.

SUBSTITUTION TIP: If raspberry jam and orange zest isn't your, well, jam, use your favorite flavors instead. Some of my favorite combos are strawberry jam + lemon zest, blackberry jam + vanilla extract, apricot jam + almond extract, or blueberry jam + lime zest. Homemade or sugar-free jam, or preserves all work great in this recipe.

Sun-Dried Tomato Pesto Pasta Salad with Chicken, Olives + Feta

1 pound farfalle or penne pasta (whole-wheat, white, or gluten-free)

½ cup jarred sun-dried tomatoes, drained

½ cup Parmesan cheese

2 garlic cloves, peeled

1 tablespoon dried basil or 1 cup fresh basil leaves

½ cup plus 1 tablespoon extra-virgin olive oil

1 pound boneless, skinless chicken breast, cut into bite-size pieces

Juice of 1 lemon

½ cup sliced black olives

½ cup crumbled feta cheese

SERVES 8

STORAGE
4 days in refrigerator

PREP TIME
15 minutes
COOK TIME
10 minutes

nut free

gluten free

Bring a large pot of salted water to a boil over high heat and cook the pasta according to the package directions. Reserve ½ cup of the cooking water, drain the pasta, and set aside.

In a food processor or blender, make the pesto by combining the sun-dried tomatoes, Parmesan, garlic, and basil and pulse until incorporated. Turn the machine on high and slowly drizzle in ½ cup of olive oil and run the processor for 60 to 90 seconds, scraping down the sides of the bowl if needed.

In a large skillet, heat the remaining 1 tablespoon of olive oil over medium heat. Add the chicken and cook for 5 minutes, flip, and cook until the chicken is cooked all the way through, 3 to 5 minutes more.

Add the sun-dried tomato pesto, lemon juice, and reserved pasta cooking water to the chicken and stir until combined. Add the pasta and olives and toss to combine. Sprinkle with the feta and serve. This dish is great warm or cold. If packing for lunch, it should be cold before adding to a bento or served warm in a thermos.

INGREDIENT TIP: I love adding nuts to my pesto, but because I will pack the leftovers of this recipe for Ellie's school lunch or take this pasta dish to parties where there might be kids with nut allergies, I usually leave them out of my pesto. But that doesn't mean you can't use them. Simply add ¼ cup toasted almonds or pine nuts to the food processor in step 2 and blend with the rest of the ingredients.

Even super parents need some backup every once in a while. Enter my favorite fast and healthy bento box hero: the pita pizza! Made in less than 15 minutes, these pizzas are healthy, delicious, and likely your kids' favorite lunch of the week. While I usually use pita pockets, which I always have on hand, you can also use lavash, pre-made individual-size crusts, flatbread, English muffins, or even naan for these pizzas. Topped with pesto, corn, zucchini, sweet peppers, chicken, and spinach, these pizzas go beyond the average cheese pizza selection but are still so tasty that your kids won't stop asking for them—like every day, of every week, of every month. Since these pizzas are piled high with veggies and are super filling, a simple sweet berry salad is the only additional side you need to pack.

Pesto, Corn + Zucchini Pizza

2 large pita pockets, 1 lavash (cut in half), or 2 small pre-made crusts

2 tablespoons Basil + Lemon Pesto (page 162) or favorite prepared pesto

½ medium zucchini, thinly sliced

½ cup shredded mozzarella cheese

2 tablespoons corn, fresh or frozen and thawed

1 teaspoon dried parsley

½ teaspoon red pepper flakes (optional)

MAKES
2 INDIVIDUAL
PIZZAS

STORAGE
2 days in
refrigerator

PREP TIME
5 minutes
COOK TIME
15 minutes
COOL TIME
10 minutes

veg

nut
free

Preheat the oven to 425°F. Line a baking sheet with aluminum foil.

Place the crusts of choice on the baking sheet and bake for 3 to 5 minutes.

Let cool slightly, then top with a thin layer of pesto, followed by the zucchini, mozzarella, and corn. Sprinkle with the parsley and red pepper flakes (if using).

Bake until the crust is golden brown and the cheese is melted, 7 to 9 minutes. Transfer the pizzas to a cutting board and let cool for 2 minutes. Cut each pizza into 8 wedges and serve. If packing in a bento, cool the pizza wedges completely, about 10 minutes.

INGREDIENT TIP: Another one of my girls' favorite pizza combinations is to top the pesto with shredded mozzarella, sliced black olives, chopped cherry tomatoes, and a sprinkle of feta cheese.

Sweet Peppers + Cheese Pizza

**MAKES
2 INDIVIDUAL
PIZZAS**

STORAGE
2 days in
refrigerator

PREP TIME
5 minutes
COOK TIME
15 minutes
COOL TIME
10 minutes

veg

nut
free

2 large pita pockets, 1 lavash (cut in half), or 2 small pre-made crusts

½ cup Simple Pizza Sauce (page 58) or store-bought sauce

¼ teaspoon garlic powder

¼ teaspoon dried oregano

½ cup shredded mozzarella cheese

⅓ cup chopped sweet peppers

Preheat the oven to 425°F. Line a baking sheet with aluminum foil.

Place the crusts of choice on the baking sheet and bake for 3 to 5 minutes.

Let cool slightly, then top with a thin layer of pizza sauce. Evenly sprinkle the garlic powder and oregano over the sauce and then top with the mozzarella, followed by the sweet peppers.

Bake until the crust is golden brown and the cheese is melted, 7 to 9 minutes. Transfer the pizzas to a cutting board and let cool for 2 minutes. Cut each pizza into 8 wedges and serve. If packing in a bento, cool the pizza wedges completely, about 10 minutes.

SUBSITUTION TIP: This recipe is super simple and made to adjust to whatever you have in your fridge, and whatever your kids like. Feel free to sub the sweet peppers out for halved cherry tomatoes, olives, green peppers, pineapple, ham, cooked sausage, mushrooms, red peppers, or anything else you have on hand.

Chicken + Ranch Pizza with Spinach + Tomatoes

2 large pita pockets, 1 lavash (cut in half), or 2 small pre-made crusts

¼ cup Healthy Ranch Dip (page 162) or store-bought ranch dip

⅓ cup finely chopped spinach

¼ cup cubed or shredded cooked chicken

½ cup shredded mozzarella cheese

¼ cup halved cherry tomatoes

MAKES
2 INDIVIDUAL
PIZZAS

STORAGE
2 days in
refrigerator

PREP TIME
5 minutes
COOK TIME
15 minutes
COOL TIME
10 minutes

nut
free

Preheat the oven to 425°F. Line a baking sheet with aluminum foil.

Place the crusts of choice on the baking sheet and bake for 3 to 5 minutes.

Let them cool slightly, then top with a thin layer of ranch dip. Evenly scatter the spinach and chicken on top of the ranch. Sprinkle with the cheese and top with the cherry tomatoes.

Bake until the crust is golden brown and the cheese is melted, 7 to 9 minutes. Transfer the pizzas to a cutting board and let cool for 2 minutes. Cut each pizza into 8 wedges and serve. If packing in a bento, cool the pizza wedges completely, about 10 minutes.

When Parker was just a baby, I ate this nut-free (yes, nut-free!) pesto and turkey rollup all the time! Breakfast, lunch, before-dinner snack, and especially in the middle of the night—all times were fair game. I still turn to it as a lifesaver for myself and the girls when we're having a crazy morning and I need to pack something nutritious and protein-rich in a snap. The basic recipe has all the flavor it needs, but I also list a few optional healthy additions if you have some veggies on hand and a couple of extra minutes to prep. Mandarin oranges—which include clementines and tangerines—are a perfectly juicy seasonal fruit to give a little citrus kick.

Pesto + Turkey Tortilla Rollup

2 tablespoons Basil + Lemon Pesto (page 162) or store-bought pesto

1 large tortilla (white, whole-wheat, or gluten-free)

3 deli turkey slices

2 white Cheddar or provolone cheese slices

2 tablespoons shredded carrots (optional)

1 tablespoon finely sliced red bell pepper (optional)

2 slices cooked, crisp bacon (optional)

SERVES 1

PREP TIME
5 minutes

nut free

gluten free

Spread the pesto all the way to the edges of the tortilla.

Cut the turkey slices into strips and line up the pieces in the center of the tortilla. Layer the turkey with the cheese. If using, layer the carrots, red peppers, and bacon on top of the cheese. Roll the tortilla tightly and cut into 1-inch pinwheels.

SUBSTITUTION TIP: Don't have pesto in the fridge? No problem—you can use any hummus (such as the Roasted Carrot + Cumin Hummus on page 41), cream cheese mixed with a squeeze of lemon and a dash of dried oregano, Healthy Ranch Dip or Dressing (page 162) or bottled ranch dressing, or even a mixture of mayo and mustard if your fridge is beyond bare.

Spring

By the time Spring rolls around, I start to dream about fresh asparagus, red raspberries, and flavorful herbs, but I sure am tired of
packing lunches at this point in the school year. We all tend to
fall into the pb&j trap at some point, serving it 4 out of the 5 days
of the week. When you hit a rough patch in your lunch-making
creativity, turn to this chapter to find at least one fun new recipe
to add to the mix.

I often turn to my Instagram feed to see what other amazing moms are whipping up for lunch. This tuna salad comes from Debbie Comish (@lunchingdaily). It is now a staple in our house, and even appeals to kids (or adults, like me) who aren't big fans of the typically overpowering and overdressed tuna salad. This is more of a slaw salad, as tuna is mixed with shredded cabbage, carrots, and apples and lightly tossed in a Dijon-flavored dressing. Served in between cucumber slices with olives on a stick, in a pita, or with crackers, it will surely be a new favorite in your household as well. For the non-tuna eaters out there, try the Curried Chickpea Salad (page 99) instead. It's just as delicious. Whichever way you go, pack the bento with herbed popcorn and fresh raspberries—you'll get no complaints.

Tuna Slaw + Cucumber + Olive Sandwiches on a Stick

FOR THE TUNA SLAW

1 (5-ounce) can water-packed tuna, drained

1 cup finely chopped cabbage

½ cup shredded or julienned carrots

¼ cup shredded or julienned apple

2 tablespoons mayonnaise

1 tablespoon Dijon mustard

1 tablespoon apple cider vinegar

Salt

Freshly ground black pepper

FOR THE SANDWICHES ON A STICK

1 cucumber, thinly sliced

12 pitted black olives

MAKES 6 TO 8 STICK SANDWICHES WITH 1 CUP LEFTOVER TUNA SLAW

STORAGE (tuna slaw only): 3 days in refrigerator

PREP TIME 10 minutes

nut free

dairy free

gluten free

In a medium bowl, make the slaw by breaking up the tuna up with a fork. Add the cabbage, carrot, and apple and mix well.

In a small bowl, whisk together the mayonnaise, mustard, vinegar, salt, and pepper. Pour the dressing over the tuna and vegetable mixture and stir to combine.

To make the sandwiches on a stick, layer the cucumber slices between two paper towels to soak up any moisture. Spoon 1 tablespoon tuna slaw on one cucumber slice and top the "sandwich" with another cucumber slice. Repeat for the remaining cucumber slices. Thread one cucumber sandwich on a wooden skewer, followed by an olive. Each skewer will likely take 3 sandwiches and 3 olives (alternated on the skewer). Pack in a bento with an ice pack.

SUBSTITUTION TIP: It's easy to make changes to this recipe to suit your kid's taste, or yours. Not a tuna lover? This salad works great with 1 cup cooked or canned chicken, too. Miss the carbs? Feel free to forget the stick and use regular sandwich bread, mini pita pockets, crescents, or crackers.

Herbed Parmesan Popcorn

SERVES 6

STORAGE
4 days in airtight container

PREP TIME
5 minutes

veg

nut free

gluten free

6 cups air-popped popcorn

4 tablespoons unsalted butter

2 teaspoons dried parsley

½ teaspoon dried Italian seasoning blend

½ teaspoon salt

¼ teaspoon garlic powder

½ cup grated Parmesan cheese, divided

Let the freshly air-popped popcorn cool slightly in a large bowl or clean paper bag.

In a small microwave-safe bowl, melt the butter in the microwave in 20-second intervals until melted. Add the parsley, Italian seasoning, salt, and garlic powder and stir to combine. Drizzle half of the herb butter over the popcorn, sprinkle with half of the Parmesan, and stir or toss until combined. Repeat with the remaining butter and Parmesan.

Let cool completely and serve or store.

BONUS RECIPE: I don't have a popcorn maker (even though I secretly want one), so instead I make it on my stovetop. Heat 1 tablespoon coconut, peanut, or canola oil in a large saucepan over medium heat and add 3 popcorn kernels; cover the pot. When the 3 kernels have popped, add ½ cup popcorn kernels to the pan, cover, and remove the pan from the heat. Hold the lid tightly and shake like crazy for 30 full seconds. Return the pan to the heat and let the popcorn start popping. The kernels should pop roughly at the same time. When the popping starts, gently shake the pan once so the kernels at the bottom don't burn. When there is a 4-second lull between pops, the popcorn is done.

Curried Chickpea Salad

1 (15-ounce) can chickpeas, rinsed and drained

½ cup diced celery

¼ cup diced red onion

½ cup cashew pieces

3 tablespoons mayonnaise

1 tablespoon apple cider vinegar

Juice of ½ lemon

½ teaspoon Dijon mustard

½ teaspoon curry powder

Salt

Freshly ground black pepper

**MAKES
2 CUPS OR
6 SANDWICHES**

STORAGE
5 days in refrigerator

PREP TIME
10 minutes

veg

dairy free

gluten free

In a medium bowl, smash the chickpeas with the back of a fork. Mix in the celery, red onion, and cashews.

In a small bowl, whisk together the mayonnaise, vinegar, lemon juice, mustard, curry powder, salt, and pepper. Pour the dressing over the chickpeas and mix until combined.

Serve or pack into a bento.

BONUS RECIPE: This curried chickpea salad can be served between two slices of bread, with crackers, in a pita pocket, or between two cucumber slices, but one of my favorite ways to serve it is in a wrap. As much as my girls don't love bread, they do love eating pinwheel sandwiches. Go figure. Spread 2 teaspoons mayonnaise over the entire surface of a tortilla. Spoon 2 heaping tablespoons of chickpea salad down the middle, sprinkle with 1 tablespoon shredded radishes and 4 mandarin oranges (drained), roll up tightly, and cut into 1-inch pinwheels. I make myself the same wrap but add 1 handful shredded spinach and 1 tablespoon sprouts. Pinwheels are optional!

Even though my girls haven't gone through the inevitable princess phase (yet), I still lovingly refer to these carrot and beet sandwiches as Princess Sandwiches because they are pink—like, really, *really* pink. And when going for something this cute, we might as well go for full-on cuteness, so I usually cut them into small finger sandwiches or use a cookie cutter shaped like a flower or crown. But nothing, and I mean nothing, is as good as these whole-wheat seed butter cookies. They are as dunkable and crave-worthy as an Oreo. They go so fast in my house, I usually double the recipe and freeze some for a yummy after-school snack. And with sweet potato chips, blueberries, and cut green beans with ranch dip, this is one delightful bento.

Carrot + Beet Cream Cheese Sandwiches

¼ cup shredded carrots

¼ cup shredded peeled beets

4 ounces cream cheese

1 teaspoon honey

Juice of ½ lemon

⅛ teaspoon ground nutmeg

4 to 6 slices bread

MAKES ½ CUP SPREAD

STORAGE
5 days in refrigerator

PREP TIME
10 minutes

veg

nut free

Combine the carrots, beets, cream cheese, honey, lemon juice, and nutmeg in a blender or food processor. Pulse until combined but still slightly chunky, about 45 seconds.

Spread a layer of the cream cheese mixture on one slice of bread, top with another slice, and cut into halves, strips, or squares. Repeat with the remaining cream cheese mixture and bread slices. I find this makes three full sandwiches with a thin layer of cream cheese spread, or two sandwiches with a thick layer of spread. Needless to say, I make it with a thick layer for myself and a thin layer for the kiddos.

INGREDIENT TIP: The cream cheese spread is also great with crackers or cut vegetables, or rolled up in a tortilla or lavash.

BONUS RECIPE: For a fun green version of this sandwich, blend together 1 packed cup spinach, 1 tablespoon chopped fresh chives, 4 ounces cream cheese, juice of ½ lemon, and ¼ teaspoon ground cumin until the spinach is smooth, about 45 seconds (you may need the juice of another ½ lemon to get things really smooth).

Baked Sweet Potato Chips

SERVES 4

STORAGE
3 days in a
partially open
container

PREP TIME
10 minutes
COOK TIME
25 minutes

vegan

nut
free

dairy
free

gluten
free

Cooking spray

2 orange sweet potatoes, peeled

2 purple sweet potatoes, peeled

2 teaspoons extra-virgin olive oil, divided

½ teaspoon ground cumin

Salt

Preheat the oven to 375°F and place the oven racks in the top third and bottom third of the oven. Spray two baking sheets with cooking spray and set aside.

Using a mandoline, cut the sweet potatoes into ⅛- or ¹⁄₁₆-inch-thick slices. Both work great in this recipe.

Put the orange sweet potato slices in a large bowl, drizzle with half of the olive oil, and sprinkle with half of the cumin. Mix with your hands, making sure to coat all the potato slices. Spread out the slices in a single layer on one baking sheet and sprinkle with salt.

Repeat steps 2 and 3 with the purple sweet potatoes. (I like to keep the orange and purple sweet potatoes on separate baking sheets because the orange ones take a couple more minutes to bake than the purple ones.)

Bake for 15 minutes, then check for doneness. Continue baking until the potatoes are crispy and gently golden brown. Some edges might begin to burn a little because of uneven slicing; take those out earlier while the remaining potatoes bake. The purple sweet potatoes will take about 20 minutes, while the orange sweet potatoes will take about 25 minutes.

Let the chips cool for 10 minutes on the baking sheet. They will continue to crisp up as they cool. If packing in a bento, cool completely.

SUBSTITUTION TIP: This recipe can be used for any root chips—golden beets, red beets, parsnips, turnips, etc. The only variation is the cooking times, so play around with your favorite root veggies to come up with your family's favorite variety!

Seed Butter Cookies

¾ cup white whole-wheat or all-purpose flour

½ cup whole-wheat flour

¾ teaspoon baking soda

½ teaspoon baking powder

½ teaspoon ground cinnamon

½ teaspoon salt

½ cup Seed Butter (page 77) or store-bought

½ cup unsalted butter, at room temperature

½ cup brown sugar

⅓ cup granulated sugar

1 large egg

MAKES
36 MINI
COOKIES OR
18 REGULAR-
SIZE

FREEZER
FRIENDLY

STORAGE
5 days in
airtight
container,
2 months
in freezer

PREP TIME
10 minutes
CHILL TIME
1 to 12 hours
COOK TIME
10 minutes

veg

nut
free

In a medium bowl, whisk together the flours, baking soda, baking powder, cinnamon, and salt.

In a large bowl or the bowl of a stand mixer, cream the seed butter, butter, and sugars for 2 minutes. Add the egg and beat for another minute.

Add the dry ingredients to the wet ingredients on medium-low speed, just until combined. Cover the bowl with plastic wrap and chill in the refrigerator for at least 1 hour, but preferably overnight. If not chilled first, the cookies will spread to the point of no return while baking.

Preheat the oven to 375°F. Line two baking sheets with parchment paper.

Roll the dough into balls, 1 tablespoon for regular-size cookies or 1 teaspoon for mini cookies, and place on the lined baking sheets. If the dough sticks to your hands, wet your hands with cold water first and then roll the dough into balls. Using a fork, press down into each ball to create crisscross marks. This is easier if the fork is wet.

Bake until golden brown, 9 to 11 minutes. Let cool for 2 minutes on the baking sheet and then transfer to a wire rack to cool completely.

SUBSTITUTION TIP: This recipe works great for any nut or seed butter you have on hand—sunflower seed butter, almond butter, peanut butter, or even cashew butter.

I was skeptical at first about making my own fruit leathers—they take 3 hours. Is it really worth it? Absolutely. Even the healthier fruit leather brands are full of refined sugar and ingredients you can't pronounce. But it is the taste of these homemade leathers that will keep you making them each weekend. The first time I made this flavor, I took half of the batch to a park play date with Ellie's best friend and the kids ate them all before I could blink. Then they started asking for more, more, more! The only reason I hadn't brought the entire batch was because I had already eaten it when it came out of the oven. (Quality control at its finest.) So, the fruit leather may be the first thing to go in a bento, but there will be no complaints with the apple cranberry chicken salad, slices of cucumber and bell peppers, fresh corn, and a handful of blueberries.

Apple + Cranberry Chicken Salad

¼ cup plain Greek yogurt, 2% or full-fat

¼ cup mayonnaise

1 tablespoon whole-grain mustard

1 teaspoon honey

1 teaspoon chopped fresh parsley

½ teaspoon ground cumin

Salt

Freshly ground black pepper

2 cups diced or shredded cooked chicken

1 apple, cored and finely chopped

¼ cup chopped pecans (optional)

2 tablespoons roughly chopped dried cranberries

SERVES 4

STORAGE
1 week in refrigerator

PREP TIME
10 minutes

nut free

gluten free

In a medium bowl, whisk together the yogurt, mayonnaise, mustard, honey, parsley, cumin, salt, and pepper. Add the chicken, apple, pecans (if using), and cranberries and mix until well incorporated. Serve alongside crackers, in a pita, or between two slices of bread.

INGREDIENT TIP: The mix of mayonnaise and Greek yogurt works perfectly to make this healthier version of chicken salad. I have also used only Greek yogurt with a splash of lemon juice for equally delicious results. The key here is that you need to use 2% or full-fat Greek yogurt so the salad has some fatty goodness to it and binds together. Serve the chicken salad as is, or between two slices of bread, in a pita, with crackers, or in a tortilla as a wrap.

Raspberry + Lemon Fruit Leather

12 ounces frozen raspberries, thawed

Juice of 1 lemon

½ teaspoon grated lemon zest

3 tablespoons honey

MAKES
16 STRIPS

STORAGE
1 month
in airtight
container

PREP TIME
5 minutes
COOK TIME
3 hours

veg

nut
free

dairy
free

gluten
free

Preheat the oven to 170°F, or the lowest temperature on your oven. Line a baking sheet with a silicone baking mat or parchment paper.

Combine all the ingredients in a blender or food processor and blend until the mixture is smooth, about 1 minute, scraping down the sides of the bowl if needed.

You can remove the raspberry seeds by pressing the mixture through a fine-mesh strainer. If you don't mind the seeds, skip this step.

Pour the mixture onto the lined baking sheet and spread in a thin, even layer, roughly ⅛ inch thick, all the way to the edges of the mat or paper. I find that tilting and gently tapping the baking sheet on the counter works great for getting an even layer.

Bake until you can touch the leather and it's no longer wet but still slightly tacky, 2½ to 3 hours. The baking time will vary depending on the thickness of the layer and the temperature of your oven. If your oven only goes down to 200°F, then opening your oven door for 15 seconds every 30 minutes helps the leather dry out. Let cool completely.

Transfer the cooled leather to a fresh piece of parchment paper and cut the leather and paper into 1-inch strips with scissors, a pizza cutter, or a sharp knife. Roll up in the parchment paper and store in an airtight container.

SUBSTITUTION TIP: This recipe is very versatile, so mix it up with whatever is in season or in your freezer. Just keep the weight of the fruit to around 12 ounces and the amounts of lemon juice and honey the same, and you will have countless fruit leather options at your disposal. Some of my favorites are peach + basil, strawberry + mint, and pear + cinnamon.

Southwest Chicken Salad

¼ cup mayonnaise

¼ cup plain Greek yogurt, 2% or full-fat

Juice of 1 lime

2 tablespoons mild or medium salsa (optional)

½ teaspoon garlic powder

½ teaspoon chili powder

½ teaspoon ground cumin

½ teaspoon salt

2 cups diced or shredded cooked chicken

½ cup canned black beans, rinsed and drained

½ cup corn, thawed if frozen

3 tablespoons finely chopped fresh cilantro

SERVES 4

STORAGE
1 week in refrigerator

PREP TIME:
10 minutes

nut free

gluten free

In a medium bowl, whisk together the mayonnaise, yogurt, lime juice, salsa (if using), garlic powder, chili powder, cumin, and salt. Add the chicken, black beans, corn, and cilantro and mix until well incorporated. Serve alongside crackers, in a pita, between two slices of bread, or even on top of nachos (see tip below).

MAKE IT A MEAL: You can certainly serve this chicken salad as is or in a sandwich, but I used it as a topping for a quickly thrown together nacho dish one busy weekday night. It sounds crazy, but it was beyond delicious. To make, spread a thin layer of tortilla chips on a foil-lined baking sheet, sprinkle with a serving of the chicken salad, then add a layer of Mexican-blend cheese and put under the broiler until the cheese is golden brown and the chips are almost burnt, about 10 minutes. Let cool slightly and then scatter 1 chopped avocado and ½ cup chopped cherry tomatoes over the top.

Bahn mi is a Vietnamese sandwich loaded with pork, chicken, or tofu; pickled vegetables; mayonnaise; and cilantro on an airy, fluffy roll. Since my girls are bread averse, I popped the traditional bahn mi ingredients onto a stick and then whipped together a cilantro dipping sauce. This recipe takes some time to make, so unless you are an early bird, I absolutely recommend you make this for a family dinner and then serve the leftovers for lunch later in the week. With spiced chickpeas, bell pepper strips, and fresh blackberries, raspberries, and tangerines, you can send your kids on a culinary tour of the world without leaving school.

Tofu Bahn Mi on a Stick

FOR THE QUICK-PICKLED
VEGETABLES

1 cup water

¼ cup rice vinegar or white vinegar

2 tablespoons sugar

2 teaspoons salt

2 carrots, thinly sliced

1 red bell pepper, seeded and cut
into squares

1 daikon, cucumber, or jicama, peeled
and thinly sliced

½ jalapeño pepper, seeded and sliced
(optional)

FOR THE TOFU

1 (14-ounce) package extra-firm tofu

2 tablespoons tamari or reduced-
sodium soy sauce

1 tablespoon toasted sesame oil

Juice of ½ lime

1 garlic clove, minced

½ teaspoon grated fresh ginger

½ teaspoon ground cumin

Freshly ground black pepper

1 tablespoon extra-virgin olive oil

FOR THE SANDWICH ON A STICK

1 large crusty roll, cut into 1-inch cubes

MAKES
12 SANDWICHES
ON A STICK
OR 4 LARGE
SANDWICHES
ON ROLLS

STORAGE
(tofu): 5 days
in refrigerator,
(pickled
vegetables):
1 month in
refrigerator

PREP TIME
45 minutes
MARINATING
TIME
30 minutes
COOK TIME
15 minutes

veg

nut
free

dairy
free

In a small saucepan, make the brine for the vegetables by bringing the water, vinegar, sugar, and salt to a soft boil. Stir until the sugar and salt dissolve.

Pack the carrots, bell pepper, daikon, and jalapeño (if using) in a glass jar with an airtight lid. Pour the brine over them, making sure they are completely covered, close the lid, and refrigerate for at least 30 minutes.

Meanwhile, remove the tofu from the package and pat it dry with a paper towel to remove any excess water. Cut the tofu into 1-inch cubes.

In a medium bowl, whisk together the tamari, sesame oil, lime juice, garlic, ginger, cumin, and pepper. Add the tofu and mix gently until the cubes are coated with the sauce. Let the tofu marinate for at least 10 minutes or up to 8 hours in the refrigerator, if needed.

In a large skillet, heat the olive oil over medium-high heat. Add the tofu and cook for about 3 minutes per side, flipping until all sides are golden brown and crispy, 12 to 15 minutes total. Remove from the heat and let cool on a paper towel.

To make each sandwich, alternate layers of pickled vegetables, tofu, and bread on a wooden skewer. Or, serve tofu and vegetables on a crusty roll. Either way, serve with Cilantro Dipping Sauce (page 110).

Cilantro Dipping Sauce

MAKES
½ CUP

STORAGE
1 week in
refrigerator

PREP TIME
5 minutes

veg

nut
free

dairy
free

gluten
free

1 cup fresh cilantro leaves

2 garlic cloves, peeled

1 teaspoon grated fresh ginger

½ jalapeño pepper, seeded

1 tablespoon honey

¼ teaspoon salt

¼ cup extra-virgin olive oil

2 tablespoons apple cider vinegar

In a food processor or blender, combine the cilantro, garlic, ginger, jalapeño, honey, and salt and start blending. With the machine running on high speed, slowly drizzle in the olive oil and apple cider vinegar. Continue to blend on high for 1 minute for a smooth dipping sauce, or pulse until combined for a chunkier sauce.

MAKE IT A MEAL: I love this dressing with just about anything and everything you can think of using a dip for, but especially in a chopped salad with avocado, broccoli, and bacon. To make the salad, combine 6 cups chopped spring salad mix, 1 small chopped green apple, ½ small diced cucumber, 3 slices crumbled crisp bacon, 3 sliced scallions, 1 cup broccoli florets, and ⅓ cup pistachios in a large bowl and toss. The key to a good chopped salad is to chop all the ingredients into bite-size pieces. Gently toss in 1 chopped avocado and ⅓ cup crumbled feta cheese and drizzle with 2 tablespoons cilantro dipping sauce. This makes 2 large salads. For the girls, I set out pieces of each ingredient so they can dip them in the dressing.

Crunchy Moroccan-Spiced Chickpeas

1 (15-ounce) can chickpeas, rinsed and drained

¼ teaspoon salt

¼ teaspoon curry powder

¼ teaspoon ground cumin

⅛ teaspoon ground cinnamon

⅛ teaspoon ground coriander

Pinch ground cloves

Pinch cayenne pepper (optional)

Cooking spray

SERVES 4

STORAGE
5 days in airtight container

PREP TIME
5 minutes
COOK TIME
30 minutes

vegan

nut free

dairy free

gluten free

Preheat the oven to 425°F.

Thoroughly dry the chickpeas by laying them on a stack of paper towels and gently rolling them around. If they are wet, they won't get as crispy. Place them in a single layer on a baking sheet and roast, giving the pan a shake every 10 minutes, until the chickpeas are golden brown, crispy on the outside, and still soft on the inside, 30 to 40 minutes.

Meanwhile, in a small bowl, mix the salt, curry, cumin, cinnamon, coriander, cloves, and cayenne pepper (if using).

As soon as the chickpeas come out of the oven, coat them lightly with cooking spray and then sprinkle with the spices. Toss to coat. Leave the chickpeas to cool on the baking sheet. They will continue to get crunchy as they cool. Cool completely before packing in a bento.

TIP: Besides snacking on them, I use these crispy chickpeas in a salad in lieu of croutons, or on top of a creamy soup for a little crunch.

The first time I made these chicken strips, I left the room for a couple of minutes while they were cooling on the counter. When I came back, Ellie and Parker were eating the chicken straight off the pan! Thank goodness the pan was only slightly warm at that point. Needless to say, this recipe has become a staple in our home, along with the delicious honey-mustard dipping sauce I always pair it with. I usually make a double batch of the chicken so we can have some for dinner and then use the rest later in the week—chopped into salads, wrapped in a tortilla along with some spinach, or straight out of the fridge as is. Roasted asparagus and fresh-cut strawberries are the perfect springtime complements—bright, healthy, and easy for small hands to pick up and eat.

Crispy Chicken Strips

¼ cup sunflower seeds

2 cups crispy brown rice cereal

2 large eggs

1 tablespoon tamari or reduced-sodium soy sauce

1 teaspoon ground cumin

1 teaspoon salt, plus additional for seasoning

½ teaspoon freshly ground black pepper

1 pound boneless, skinless chicken breasts or chicken tenders

Cooking spray

SERVES 4

FREEZER FRIENDLY

STORAGE
5 days in refrigerator, 1 month in freezer

PREP TIME
15 minutes
COOK TIME
25 minutes

nut free

dairy free

gluten free

Preheat the oven to 425°F. Place a wire rack over a baking sheet and set aside.

In a small pan, toast the sunflower seeds, stirring frequently, until browned, 5 to 7 minutes. Place the seeds on a paper towel or plate and let them cool completely.

Put the crispy rice cereal in a plastic bag or food processor, and smash or pulse until the cereal is about half its original volume.

In a medium bowl, whisk together the eggs and tamari. In another medium bowl, stir together the smashed rice cereal, toasted sunflower seeds, cumin, salt, and pepper.

Cut the chicken breasts into strips or chunks and pat dry with a paper towel. Piece by piece, dip a chicken strip into the egg mixture, then toss it into the rice cereal mixture, making sure to press the cereal firmly into the chicken to get a nice thick coat on it. Place each coated chicken piece on the wire rack. When all the chicken is coated, spray them lightly with cooking spray and sprinkle with a pinch of salt.

Bake until cooked all the way through, about 20 minutes. For a darker, browned crust, place the chicken under the broiler for an additional 3 to 5 minutes, watching very closely so they don't burn.

Let cool slightly and serve, or let cool completely before packing in a bento.

PREP TIP: To freeze, cover the baking sheet with plastic wrap and transfer to the freezer overnight. Then transfer the chicken strips to a zip-top plastic bag and store for up to 1 month. To reheat, bake for 25 minutes at 350°F.

Honey-Mustard Dipping Sauce

MAKES
½ CUP

STORAGE
1 week in
refrigerator

PREP TIME
5 minutes

veg

nut
free

gluten
free

¼ cup plain Greek yogurt, 2% or full-fat

2 tablespoons yellow or Dijon mustard

2 tablespoons raw honey (see tip)

⅛ teaspoon sea salt

¼ teaspoon freshly ground
black pepper

In a small bowl, whisk together all the ingredients until smooth. If packing in a bento, include an ice pack.

INGREDIENT TIP: This dipping sauce won't work with a thin or runny honey. I prefer to use raw honey because it's thicker than the refined honey that's typically stocked on supermarket shelves. I've also made it with organic (but not raw) honey and it turned out well. For best results, skip the cheap stuff. If your dip is runnier than you'd like simply refrigerate it for at least 10 minutes to help it firm up before serving. I also love adding 1 tablespoon finely chopped fresh chives to my honey mustard for a fun kick.

Easy Pan-Roasted Asparagus + Rosemary

1½ teaspoons unsalted butter

1 cup sliced asparagus (3-inch pieces)

⅛ teaspoon crushed dried rosemary

Salt

Freshly ground black pepper

SERVES 2

STORAGE
3 days in
refrigerator

PREP TIME
5 minutes
COOK TIME
5 minutes

veg

nut
free

gluten
free

In a small skillet, heat the butter over medium heat. Add the asparagus and cook, stirring often, until bright green and still crisp, 3 to 4 minutes.

Remove the pan from the heat and sprinkle the asparagus with the rosemary, salt, and pepper, stirring in the pan for 1 more minute. Serve warm or let cool completely before adding to a bento box.

SUBSTITUTION TIP: This easy pan-roasting method works for a bunch of different vegetable and spice pairings: broccoli + chives, green beans + lemon zest, cauliflower + coriander, zucchini + cumin, squash + nutmeg, and red peppers + cilantro. The only thing you might need to change is the roasting time, as some denser veggies, like broccoli and cauliflower, take a couple of minutes longer.

I probably shouldn't admit it, but this is my favorite box of the season. A veggie-loaded pasta salad with cooked but still-tender asparagus, yellow squash, peas, and pine nuts all tossed together in a fresh pesto—what's not to love? Because this pasta is at its best when served cold, it's ideal for school lunches. Pair it with crunchy honey-mustard pretzels and to-die-for brownies and you could (and just might) serve this lunch every day of the week without any complaints. Just toss some cherry tomato halves and orange slices into the bento. And, if you're anything like me, the brownies pair exceptionally well with a bold cabernet sauvignon, perfect for a late-night grown-up snack.

Spring Veggie + Mint Pesto Pasta Salad

1 (16-ounce) package pasta, such as rotini, farfalle, penne

1½ cups fresh basil leaves

½ cup fresh mint leaves

1 garlic clove, peeled

½ cup Parmesan cheese

Juice of 1 lemon

Salt

Freshly ground black pepper

½ cup extra-virgin olive oil

1 cup frozen peas (no need to thaw)

1 cup chopped asparagus

1 cup chopped yellow squash or zucchini

¼ cup pine nuts, toasted

SERVES 8

STORAGE
1 week in refrigerator

PREP TIME
15 minutes
COOK TIME
10 minutes

veg

Bring a large pot of salted water to a boil over high heat and cook the pasta according to the package directions, keeping in mind that you'll add the vegetables before the cooking is complete.

Meanwhile, in a blender or food processor, make the pesto. Combine the basil, mint, garlic, Parmesan, lemon juice, salt, and pepper and pulse. With the machine running at high speed, slowly drizzle in the olive oil. Continue to blend at high speed for 1 minute, scraping down the sides of the bowl if needed.

When the pasta has 2 minutes left to cook, add the peas, asparagus, and squash to the pot. After 2 minutes, drain and immediately rinse the pasta and vegetables under cold water.

In a large bowl, toss together the pasta, vegetables, and pesto until well combined. Sprinkle in the pine nuts and serve warm or cold. If packing for lunch, chill the pasta salad completely before placing in the bento box. If you're serving leftovers later in the week, you might need to drizzle a little more olive oil over the pasta before serving, as the pasta absorbs some of the olive oil while in the refrigerator and can become dry.

BONUS RECIPE: My favorite dish to bring to spring and summer gatherings is a big bowl of caprese pesto pasta salad. It's easy to toss together and is enjoyed by kids and adults alike. To make, cook 1 pound of your favorite pasta shape according to the package directions, drain, and rinse with cold water. In a large bowl, toss together the pasta, 1 recipe Basil + Lemon Pesto (page 162), 2 cups halved cherry tomatoes, 8 (1-ounce) mini mozzarella balls, and ½ cup sliced black olives. Of course, before you head to the party, take a minute to reserve a portion for your kids' lunches later in the week. Kill two birds with one dish!

Olive Oil + Walnut Brownies

**MAKES
16 SQUARES**

FREEZER
FRIENDLY

STORAGE
1 week in
airtight
container

PREP TIME
15 minutes
COOK TIME
30 minutes

veg

Cooking spray

¼ cup white whole-wheat or
all-purpose flour

⅓ cup unsweetened cocoa powder

¼ teaspoon baking powder

¼ teaspoon salt

1 cup dark chocolate chips, divided

⅓ cup extra-virgin olive oil

½ cup sugar

2 large eggs

1 teaspoon pure vanilla extract

½ cup chopped raw walnuts

¼ teaspoon sea salt (optional)

Preheat the oven to 350°F. Line an 8-inch square pan with enough parchment paper so the edges hang over the sides of the pan, and lightly coat with cooking spray.

In a small bowl, whisk together the flour, cocoa powder, baking powder, and salt. Set aside.

In a small microwave-safe bowl, melt ⅔ cup of chocolate chips in the microwave. Transfer to a medium mixing bowl, add the olive oil, and stir until smooth. Stir in the sugar. Beat in the eggs, one at a time. Stir in the vanilla extract and beat vigorously with a wooden spoon until the batter is shiny and smooth, about 1 minute. Add the dry ingredients and mix just until combined. Stir in the remaining ⅓ cup of chocolate chips and the walnuts.

Pour the batter into the pan and spread it out evenly. Sprinkle with sea salt (if using) and bake for 30 minutes. Let cool completely before cutting into squares.

SUBSTITUTION TIP: By all means replace the walnuts with 1 cup frozen raspberries for a fruity (and nut-free) twist.

Honey-Mustard Spiced Pretzels

Cooking spray

3 tablespoons unsalted butter or coconut oil, melted

3 tablespoons honey

3 tablespoons yellow mustard

1 teaspoon Worcestershire sauce

½ teaspoon onion powder

½ teaspoon garlic powder

6 cups pretzels

SERVES 10

STORAGE
1 week in airtight container

PREP TIME
5 minutes
COOK TIME
45 minutes

veg

nut free

Preheat the oven to 250°F. Coat a baking sheet with cooking spray.

In a large bowl, stir together the butter, honey, mustard, Worcestershire sauce, onion powder, and garlic powder. Add the pretzels and toss until well coated. Spread out the pretzels in a single layer on the baking sheet.

Bake for 45 minutes, stirring the pretzels every 15 minutes. Let cool completely and serve or store.

Perfectly doughy and chewy on the inside, with a little salty crunch on the outside, these pretzel bites are where it's at, whether for a kid's party or in a school lunch. Serve them with a variety of green dippers (apple slices, snap peas, green bell pepper slices) and a slightly spicy dipping sauce. For a protein boost, pack in some simple grilled chicken strips (not pictured). If you have some extra time on your hands and your child goes crazy for the pretzel bites, consider adding a protein by making them into pretzel dogs. I like to choose uncured chicken or turkey hot dogs—bonus points if they're organic. For an alternative to the pretzels, try the Easy Baked Falafel recipe. Either way, you'll have a box full of wholesome and fun finger foods that your kids will love dipping and eating.

Easy Whole-Wheat Pretzel Bites

1 recipe Whole-Wheat Pizza Dough (page 160) or store-bought pizza dough

½ cup baking soda (optional)

1 large egg, beaten

1 teaspoon coarse sea salt and/or poppy seeds

MAKES
60 (1-INCH)
BITES

FREEZER
FRIENDLY

STORAGE
1 week in
airtight
container,
2 months in
freezer

PREP TIME
25 minutes
COOK TIME
20 minutes

veg

nut
free

dairy
free

Preheat the oven to 425°F.

On a lightly floured work surface, divide the dough into four equal pieces. Roll each piece into a 1-inch-thick rope. Use a serrated knife to cut the ropes into 1-inch pieces.

This step isn't necessary, but it does make for more pretzel flavor: Fill a large stockpot with water and add the baking soda. Bring the water to a boil over high heat, whisking until the baking soda is dissolved. Working in batches, use a large slotted spoon to lower the pretzel bites into the boiling water. Boil for 20 to 30 seconds, then remove from the water with the slotted spoon, letting all excess water drip off. Place them on a baking sheet.

Brush the beaten egg all over the pretzel bites and then sprinkle them with sea salt or poppy seeds or a mixture of both.

Bake for 10 minutes, turn the oven to broil, and broil until the bites are golden brown, 3 to 5 minutes. Remove from the oven and cool completely before packing in a bento or freezing.

COOKING TIP: To reheat frozen pretzel bites, microwave them for 45 to 60 seconds or bake in a 350°F oven for 15 to 20 minutes.

Blackberry-Mustard Dipping Sauce

MAKES
¾ CUP

STORAGE
2 weeks in
refrigerator

PREP TIME
5 minutes

veg

nut
free

dairy
free

gluten
free

3 tablespoons blackberry jam

¼ cup honey

¼ cup whole-grain mustard

½ teaspoon Sriracha

In a small bowl, whisk together all the ingredients until blended.

SUBSTITUTION TIP: For even more mustard dipping fun, raspberry or blueberry jam works just as well.

MAKE IT A MEAL: This dipping sauce makes a mean spread on a ham and cheese panini. To make lunch for two, lay out four slices of bread. Spread butter on one side of each slice, flip them over, and spread blackberry-mustard dipping sauce on the other side of each. On the blackberry-mustard side of two of the bread slices, layer ¼ cup shredded cheese or 2 slices of cheese (Gouda, mozzarella, fontina, or Gruyère are all good choices) and 4 thin slices of ham. Close the sandwiches with the remaining two bread slices, butter-side up. Grill in a panini press or in a medium skillet over medium heat for 3 minutes per side.

Easy Baked Falafel

1½ teaspoons olive oil, plus more for coating baking sheet

1 cup fresh parsley leaves

3 cloves garlic

2 teaspoons ground cumin

1 teaspoon ground coriander

1 teaspoon salt

1 (15-ounce) can chickpeas, drained and rinsed

¼ teaspoon baking soda

¼ cup panko breadcrumbs

1 egg, beaten

1 cup Lemon + Cumin Hummus (page 163), for serving

MAKES 4 SERVINGS (10 SMALL PATTIES)

STORAGE:
5 days in refrigerator

PREP TIME:
15 minutes
COOK TIME:
30 minutes

veg

nut free

dairy free

Preheat the oven to 400°F. Using a brush, generously coat a baking sheet with olive oil.

Combine the parsley, garlic, cumin, coriander, and salt in a food processor and blend for 10 to 15 seconds.

Add the chickpeas and pulse 10 times or until everything is combined and the chickpeas are still slightly chunky. Sprinkle in the baking soda, then add the breadcrumbs and egg. Pulse until everything is just incorporated, scraping down the sides of the bowl, if needed. Let sit for 10 minutes.

Form the dough into 10 small patties or balls, and place on the baking sheet. Brush the tops of the patties with 1½ teaspoons of olive oil.

Place the baking sheet in the oven and bake for 15 minutes. Flip and bake for another 15 minutes. Let cool slightly. If packing in a bento, cool completely before packing.

If eating at home, place 2 patties on each plate and serve with the hummus. To pack in a bento, add 2 patties to the box along with ¼ cup of hummus in a small container.

INGREDIENT TIP: Want to add a vegetable to this meal? Try replacing ½ cup of the parsley with ½ cup of spinach. My girls never even notice the switch!

BONUS RECIPE: To make a pita sandwich, heat half of a pita pocket until just warm and then fill it up with 2 tablespoons Lemon + Cumin Hummus, 2 falafel patties, 4 cucumber slices, 1 tablespoon chopped tomatoes, 1 teaspoon chopped red onion, and a big pour of hot sauce (for the adults).

If you have hardboiled eggs in your fridge (and of course I think you should), this egg salad comes together in 5 minutes or less. Creamy and delicious, it's one of Ellie's favorites. Add a side of store-bought or homemade crackers (try my savory Cheddar and rosemary recipe, see the Tip, page 82) as small scoopers for the salad. I like pairing the creamy salad with my crunchy "fancy" ants on a log. There is nothing wrong with the more familiar peanut butter and raisin version—I serve it for a snack all the time. But to give it a sweet twist and make it nut-free, I switch it up by using cream cheese and dried blueberries.

Curried Egg Salad

veg / nut free / gluten free

4 hardboiled eggs, roughly chopped

2 tablespoons mayonnaise

2 tablespoons plain Greek yogurt, 2% or full-fat

½ teaspoon yellow mustard

½ teaspoon curry powder

Pinch of paprika

2 teaspoons finely chopped fresh chives (optional)

Salt

Freshly ground black pepper

SERVES 2

PREP TIME
5 minutes

In a medium bowl, mash together the eggs, mayonnaise, yogurt, mustard, curry powder, paprika, and chives (if using). Season with salt and pepper. Gently stir to combine. If packing in a bento, include an ice pack.

Fancy Ants on a Log

vegan / nut free / gluten free

2 tablespoons cream cheese

1 celery rib, cut into 2-inch sections

8 blueberries, dried or fresh

SERVES 1

PREP TIME
5 minutes

Spoon the cream cheese into each celery section until full. Line up the blueberries in a row down the middle of the cream cheese, pressing down gently so they stay in place.

5

Summer

Summertime is theoretically a lazy time for our family. But of course, when I say lazy, I mean we are ridiculously busy hanging out at the pool, riding our bikes to the girls' favorite parks (which happen to be on the way to my favorite breweries), watching outdoor movies, and meeting up with friends. These bentos are filled with easy meals that are perfect for family dinners and then can be reused for lunches throughout the week. Summer is all about fresh, colorful, and flavorful produce that is ready to be enjoyed by all.

If there are two things the girls and I have in common, it's our unconditional love for Cobb salad and our horribly awkward dance moves. The salad, fortunately, is fit for public consumption. This deconstructed version of the classic Cobb is made for dipping—scrumptious rows of chicken, cucumber, hardboiled eggs, bacon, and cherry tomatoes are lined up and ready to be dunked into the most delicious feta dipping sauce. Don't get me started on this dipping sauce (or dressing, in grown-up speak) paired with a batch of homemade sweet potato fries . . . this is where food dreams come from. If your child's school doesn't have a nut-free policy, try the chicken Waldorf salad alternative sometime. Whichever you choose, a mix of blueberries and fresh peach slices complements it.

Deconstructed Cobb Salad

2 cups cubed cooked chicken or turkey

1 cucumber, quartered lengthwise and sliced crosswise

4 hardboiled eggs, diced

4 bacon slices, cooked and crumbled

¾ cup halved cherry tomatoes

3 cups chopped romaine or other mixed green salad blend (optional)

4 tablespoons Creamy Feta Dipping Sauce (page 130)

SERVES 4

STORAGE
3 days in refrigerator

PREP TIME
15 minutes

nut free

gluten free

On a plate or in a bento box, line up the chicken, cucumber, eggs, bacon, and tomatoes, each in its own row. To make this a traditional salad, serve on top of the romaine. Serve each salad with 1 tablespoon of the dipping sauce.

PREP TIP: Hardboiled eggs from the oven? Total game changer. This method is so easy and hands-off but gives you perfect eggs each time. Preheat the oven to 325°F. Place 12 eggs, still in the shell, in the cups of a regular-size or mini muffin tin. Bake the eggs for 30 minutes, then transfer them to a large bowl of ice water for 10 minutes, which stops the cooking process. Dry off and refrigerate until ready to eat.

INGREDIENT TIP: If you have a fresh avocado on hand, chop it up and add it to this salad—avocado, bacon, and feta dressing are meant to go together.

Creamy Feta Dipping Sauce

MAKES
½ CUP

STORAGE
1 week in
refrigerator

PREP-TIME
5 minutes

veg

nut
free

gluten
free

2 tablespoons milk

¼ cup mayonnaise or sour cream

1 tablespoon apple cider vinegar

1 garlic clove, minced

½ teaspoon chopped fresh dill
or ⅛ teaspoon dried dill

½ teaspoon chopped fresh oregano
or ⅛ teaspoon dried oregano

¼ cup feta cheese, crumbled

In a small bowl, whisk together the milk, mayonnaise, vinegar, garlic, dill, and oregano until well combined.

Add the feta cheese and mix it in, breaking up the larger pieces with the back of your spoon.

MAKE IT A MEAL: I use this sauce as a dressing for my favorite chopped Greek salad, which is great for a lunch or a side dish for a family dinner. In a large bowl, combine 1 (15-ounce) can rinsed and drained chickpeas, 1 pint halved cherry tomatoes, ¼ cup finely chopped red onion, 1 cup sliced Kalamata olives, and 1 chopped cucumber (seeded if you prefer). Drizzle with about half of the Creamy Feta Dipping Sauce or more to your taste. You can also toss the salad with 3 cups finely shredded spinach for a bulkier salad and serve with Toasted Spiced Pita Chips (page 42).

ALTERNATIVE MAIN

Deconstructed Chicken Waldorf Salad

2 cups cubed cooked chicken

2 sweet apples, cored and chopped

1 cup halved red seedless grapes

1 cup ½-inch celery pieces

¾ cup toasted walnuts

3 cups chopped romaine or other mixed green salad blend (optional)

4 tablespoons Creamy Feta Dipping Sauce (page 130), Healthy Ranch Dip or Dressing (page 162), or Basic Vinaigrette (page 163)

SERVES 4

STORAGE
2 days in refrigerator (apples drizzled with lemon juice)

PREP TIME
15 minutes

gluten free

On a plate or in a bento box, line up the chicken, apples, grapes, celery, and walnuts, each in its own row. To make this as a traditional salad, serve on top of the romaine. Serve each salad with 1 tablespoon of your favorite dipping sauce or dressing.

BONUS RECIPE: It's easy to turn this salad into a sandwich. In a large bowl, whisk together ¼ cup mayonnaise or plain full-fat Greek yogurt, juice of ½ lemon, 1 tablespoon finely chopped fresh chives, salt, and pepper. Then add the Waldorf salad ingredients, chopping the walnuts and celery into small pieces, and toss until combined. Spoon the salad into four large or six small pita pockets.

Summer 131

The Mais Pizza is the only thing Ellie will order at our favorite local pizza joint. It's an individual-size white pizza topped with roasted corn, thinly shaved ham, and a touch of oregano. She happily eats the entire pizza by herself! She also tries to sit at the table next to us, rather than with us, and Parker only wants to sit on my lap. So, there is that mealtime fun. With an ABC salad (apple, beet, and carrot) and a nutritious chocolate pudding, this box will be demolished in no time. *Buon appetito!*

Mais Pizza

2 large pita pockets, 1 lavash (cut in half), or 2 small pre-made crusts

½ cup crème fraîche

1 cup shredded mozzarella cheese

1 cup frozen roasted corn, thawed

4 ounces thinly sliced ham, shredded

1 teaspoon dried oregano

2 tablespoons extra-virgin olive oil

MAKES 4 (6-INCH) PIZZAS

STORAGE
3 days in refrigerator

PREP TIME
10 minutes
COOK TIME
15 minutes

nut free

Preheat the oven to 425°F. Line a baking sheet with aluminum foil.

Place the crusts of choice on the baking sheet and bake until just getting crispy, 5 to 7 minutes.

Evenly layer the crusts with the crème fraîche, scatter the mozzarella and corn on top, place small bundles of ham slices on the corn, sprinkle with the oregano, and drizzle the olive oil over the entire pizza.

Bake for 5 minutes, then turn the oven to broil, and broil until the cheese is bubbly and the crust is golden brown, 5 to 7 minutes. Let cool for a few minutes and serve. If packing in a bento, cool completely first.

INGREDIENT TIP: Most grocery stores carry frozen roasted corn, but if you can't find it, thaw regular corn and then char it in a medium skillet over medium-high heat for 5 to 7 minutes. It doesn't add quite as much roasted flavor to the pizza, but it will still be delicious. Also, if you don't have crème fraîche on hand or can't find it at the store, you can use cream cheese or sour cream.

ABC Salad with Lemon Dressing

SERVES 6

STORAGE
2 days in refrigerator (carrots and apples will turn slightly red from beets)

PREP TIME
15 minutes

veg

nut free

dairy free

gluten free

1 apple

1 small red beet

2 carrots

2 tablespoons finely chopped fresh mint

2 tablespoons apple cider vinegar

2 tablespoons extra-virgin olive oil

1 tablespoon honey

Juice of 1 lemon

1 teaspoon grated lemon zest

Salt

Freshly ground black pepper

Julienne the apple, beet, and carrots with a sharp knife or a mandoline with a ⅛-inch blade. To prevent the color of the julienned beet from leaching, rinse it under cold water for 2 to 3 minutes and then dry between a few layers of paper towels.

In a large bowl, toss together the apple, beet, carrots, and mint.

In a small bowl, whisk together the vinegar, olive oil, honey, lemon juice, lemon zest, salt, and pepper. Drizzle about half the dressing over the salad and toss to combine, adding more dressing if needed. Save any leftover dressing for a later use.

BONUS RECIPE: If your kids aren't on the beet bandwagon, just use apples and carrots. You can show off the beets in your salad and let them be jealous that you have a pink food on your plate and they don't. Try introducing just one-quarter of the julienned beets in their salads and take it slow.

Chocolate Avocado Pudding

1 ripe avocado

1 brown banana

⅔ cup almond or coconut milk

⅓ cup cocoa powder

⅓ cup maple syrup

1 teaspoon vanilla extract

⅛ teaspoon ground cinnamon

SERVES 4

STORAGE
3 days in refrigerator

PREP TIME
10 minutes
COOL TIME
1 to 2 hours

vegan

nut free

gluten free

Place the avocado, banana, almond milk, cocoa powder, maple syrup, vanilla extract, and cinnamon into a food processor or blender and run the machine for 1 to 2 minutes, scraping down the sides as needed, or until the mixture is completely creamy and smooth.

Spoon the pudding into 4 separate containers and place in the refrigerator until ready to serve. This pudding is great when chilled for 1 to 2 hours for a cold pudding, but we eat it straight out of the blender for a warmer pudding as well. If packing in a bento, place in a sealable container, and place in a lunch bag with an ice pack.

BONUS RECIPE: I love serving this with a dollop of whipped coconut cream on top. To make whipped coconut cream, chill canned coconut milk or coconut cream in the refrigerator for at least 8 hours, but preferably overnight. Open the can and pour out any clear liquid. Spoon the thick white coconut cream into a medium bowl, add 1 tablespoon sweetener (honey, powdered sugar, or maple syrup), and ½ teaspoon vanilla extract and beat with a electric mixer for 1 to 2 minutes or until fully smooth.

I know I'm a parent when I pack this lunch for my kiddos for a park picnic and then the next day I reach into my coat pocket and first get stabbed by the wooden skewer, then find half a piece of cucumber, what looks like a partially eaten piece of cheese, three rocks, a used Band-Aid, a used baby wipe, and assorted food crumbs. Sometimes I wonder why I pack such nice lunches for them, and then I remember that *I* also want to eat those lunches. I love a turkey sandwich on a stick, the crispiest apple chips I have ever eaten, and chocolaty oat balls that are a treat but still good for you. I want all of that for lunch as well, even if I end up with half of it in my pocket.

Sweet Turkey Sandwich on a Stick

2 deli turkey slices

8 cherry tomatoes

2 thick Swiss or white Cheddar cheese slices, cut into quarters

1 small cucumber, thinly sliced (16 slices)

20 dried cherries

SERVES
2 (2 STICK SANDWICHES EACH)

STORAGE Not recommended

PREP TIME
10 minutes

nut free

gluten free

Roll each turkey slice into a tight tube and then cut into four sections.

On each wooden skewer, thread on 1 cherry tomato, 1 turkey roll, 1 cheese square, 2 cucumber slices, 5 dried cherries, 2 cucumber slices, 1 more cheese square, 1 more turkey roll, and 1 more cherry tomato. Or layer anyway you find fun and exciting. Cut off the pointy end of the skewer.

BONUS RECIPE: In a rush? You can easily make this into a sandwich by quartering the tomatoes and thinly slicing the cheese and layering the ingredients between two slices of bread, filling a pita pocket, or rolling into a tortilla as a wrap. Turn the dried cherries into a delicious spread by quickly blending them with $\frac{1}{3}$ cup cream cheese or mayonnaise and spreading onto your bread of choice.

Cinnamon Apple Chips

SERVES 6

STORAGE
1 week in
airtight
container

PREP TIME
10 minutes
COOK TIME
2 hours
COOL TIME
1 hour

vegan

nut
free

dairy
free

gluten
free

Cooking spray

3 apples

3 tablespoons sugar

1 teaspoon ground cinnamon

Preheat the oven to 200°F. Lightly coat two baking sheets with cooking spray.

Thinly and evenly slice the apples (with the cores) crosswise. Using a mandoline with a ⅛- or ¹⁄₁₆-inch blade works great and ensures even baking. Evenly layer the apple slices between layers of paper towels and press to remove any excess moisture. Then arrange the slices in a single layer on the baking sheets.

In a small bowl, mix the sugar and cinnamon. Sprinkle the apples with the cinnamon sugar.

Bake for 1 hour, then flip the slices over and bake for 1 hour more. Turn off the oven and let the apple chips cool in the oven for 1 hour. Store in an airtight container.

No-Cook Chocolate Chip Energy Balls

1 cup old-fashioned oats

½ cup semisweet chocolate chips

½ cup peanut butter, seed butter, or almond butter

½ cup ground flaxseed

⅓ cup honey

⅓ cup unsweetened cocoa powder (optional)

½ teaspoon pure vanilla extract

MAKES
20 (1-INCH)
BALLS

STORAGE
1 week in
refrigerator

PREP TIME
10 minutes
CHILL TIME
30 minutes

veg

gluten
free

In a large bowl, stir together all the ingredients. Cover the bowl and chill in the refrigerator for at least 30 minutes.

Roll the dough into 1-inch balls. If the dough starts to stick to your hands, wet your hands and then roll the dough into balls.

INGREDIENT TIP: You can buy ground flaxseed at the store or grind the seeds yourself. A coffee grinder works the best, but you can also grind them in a high-powered blender for 30 seconds. Store ground flaxseed in the refrigerator so it doesn't go bad as quickly.

Before your eyes pop out of your head at this highly composed bento box, rest assured that I also give you an alternative recipe option that you can pull off in five seconds flat. If you opt for the soba noodle recipe, it's a great one for getting your kids in the kitchen to help you make dinner. After you cook the noodles, the kids chop the eggs and vegetables, and can then arrange their own bowls. Be warned that there is no chance your kids' bowls will resemble the photo in any way, but there is a 100 percent likelihood that they will eat more vegetables if they put the bowl together themselves. The side salad of strawberries, watermelon, mint, and feta is a favorite among adults and kids. Bring additional color and freshness to the bento with cut grapes and just a few chocolate-covered raisins.

Sesame Soba Noodle Salad

1 (9.5-ounce) package soba or thin udon noodles

¼ cup tamari or reduced-sodium soy sauce

¼ cup honey

1 tablespoon peanut butter or seed butter

2 teaspoons rice vinegar

1 teaspoon toasted sesame oil

1 teaspoon grated fresh ginger

1 garlic clove, minced

1 cup frozen shelled edamame, thawed

2 large carrots, coarsely grated or julienned

2 hardboiled eggs, peeled and halved

1 cup shredded red cabbage

1 large avocado, pitted, peeled, and sliced

1 tablespoon sesame seeds, toasted

SERVES 4

STORAGE
4 days in refrigerator (toppings stored separately)

PREP TIME
20 minutes
COOK TIME
10 minutes

veg

dairy free

Cook the noodles according to the package directions.

Meanwhile, in a small bowl, whisk together the tamari, honey, peanut butter, rice vinegar, sesame oil, ginger, and garlic until well combined.

When the noodles are done cooking, rinse them in cold water, drain, and transfer to a large bowl or return them to the pot. Pour in the tamari mixture and toss until all the noodles are coated.

Divide the noodles among four bowls or bento boxes, and layer the edamame, carrots, eggs, cabbage, and avocado on top. Sprinkle the sesame seeds over everything.

BENTO PACKING TIP: If you're preparing this recipe a day or more in advance, keep the noodles and the toppings separate, then assemble the morning you pack the lunch. Layer as shown or mix everything together, except the egg, before placing in the bento box.

SUBSTITUTION TIP: Don't limit yourself to the vegetables in the recipe. There are so many great add-in options for these soba noodles. Consider corn, peas, sliced red bell peppers, sprouts, chopped snap peas, cooked asparagus pieces, sautéed mushrooms, finely chopped scallions, and shaved radishes. Have fun and let the kids pick the toppings.

Watermelon + Strawberries with Feta + Mint

SERVES 4

STORAGE
2 days in
refrigerator

PREP TIME
10 minutes

veg

nut
free

gluten
free

2 cups cubed watermelon

2 cups chopped strawberries

¼ cup crumbled feta cheese

1 tablespoon finely chopped fresh mint

1 teaspoon balsamic vinegar

1 teaspoon honey

Juice of ½ lime

In a large bowl, toss together the watermelon, strawberries, feta, and mint.

In a small bowl, whisk together the vinegar, honey, and lime juice. Drizzle over the fruit and gently toss.

SUBSTITUTION TIP: Make this recipe your own. Mix it up with blueberries, chopped peaches, chopped avocado, toasted sliced almonds, sliced red onion, raspberries, or even heirloom cherry tomatoes.

Crunchy Asian Chopped Salad

FOR THE SALAD

1 (16-ounce) bag coleslaw mix

1 cup shelled edamame, thawed if frozen

1 cup shredded carrots

1 red bell pepper, julienned

¾ cup sesame sticks

⅔ cup sliced almonds, toasted

½ cup canned mandarin oranges, drained

3 green onions, thinly sliced

FOR THE DRESSING

⅓ cup olive oil

¼ cup rice wine vinegar

3 tablespoons honey

1 tablespoon reduced-sodium soy sauce

½ teaspoon sesame oil

Salt

Freshly ground black pepper

SERVES 6

STORAGE
2 days in refrigerator (dressing separate)

PREP TIME
15 minutes

veg

dairy free

In a large bowl, add all of the salad ingredients. Toss until combined.

In a small bowl, whisk together all of the dressing ingredients until combined.

Pour the dressing over the salad and mix it well before serving. If packing in a bento, pre-toss the salad with 1 tablespoon of the dressing or send the dressing on the side. This salad lasts for 2 days when tossed with the dressing, though the sesame sticks and almonds do lose some of their crunch.

INGREDIENT TIP: This is my version of the popular potluck ramen noodle salads. You can see that I substitute sesame sticks instead of the ramen noodles, but if you prefer the fun crunch of ramen noodles, feel free to add 2 packs of broken ramen noodles back in (seasoning packets removed).

Let's talk about these spinach muffins. I first made them for Ellie's entire class for a St. Patrick's Day celebration, not really knowing what 15 kids would make of green muffins. Well, they went c-r-a-z-y for them! They ate them all and wanted more—even knowing they had spinach in them. They loved the color and how bright and fun they are. Since then, I make these at least once a month, serving some right off the bat and freezing the rest. They're perfect in a bento, too, especially when paired with cottage cheese with ginger-pear sauce and an almond and dried fruit granola. Throw in some melon balls and chopped nectarines and off to school they go.

Super Green Spinach Muffins

2 cups white whole-wheat flour

⅔ cup sugar

2 teaspoons baking powder

½ teaspoon salt

2 teaspoons ground cinnamon

¼ teaspoon ground cloves

½ cup milk

½ cup extra-virgin olive oil or coconut oil, melted

⅓ cup applesauce

8 ounces frozen spinach, thawed

2 teaspoons pure vanilla extract

1 large egg

Preheat the oven to 350°F. Line 36 mini or 12 regular muffin cups with paper liners or coat with cooking spray.

In a large bowl, whisk together the flour, sugar, baking powder, salt, cinnamon, and cloves.

In a blender, blend the milk, olive oil or melted coconut oil, applesauce, spinach, and vanilla extract on high speed for 1 minute. Add the egg and blend for 10 seconds on medium speed. Pour the spinach mixture into the dry ingredients and fold together until just incorporated. Do not overmix or the muffins will become dense.

Fill the muffin cups two-thirds full. Bake until golden brown on top, 12 to 15 minutes for mini muffins or 15 to 18 for regular muffins. Let cool in the muffin tin for 5 minutes before serving. If packing in a bento, cool completely first.

SUBSTITUTION TIP: These muffins are a hit no matter which flour, sweetener, or oil you use in them. I like white whole-wheat flour because it is more nutritious than all-purpose flour but isn't as dense as whole-wheat flour tends to be in baked goods. But you can just as well substitute whole-wheat, all-purpose, or gluten-free flour. If using gluten-free, I recommend the brand Cup4Cup, which measures the same as flours with gluten. For those who avoid sugar, substitute coconut sugar or stevia. And coconut oil can easily replace olive oil, if you prefer.

Ginger-Pear Sauce over Cottage Cheese

SERVES 4

STORAGE
(pear sauce
only): 1 week
in refrigerator

PREP TIME:
5 minutes

COOK TIME
20 minutes

veg

nut
free

gluten
free

4 pears, peeled, cored, and chopped

2 teaspoons unsalted butter or coconut oil

2 tablespoons honey

1 teaspoon ground ginger

½ teaspoon ground cinnamon

½ teaspoon pure vanilla extract

2 cups plain Greek yogurt or cottage cheese, 2% or full-fat

In a small saucepan, bring the pears, butter, honey, ginger, cinnamon, and vanilla extract to a boil over medium-high heat. Reduce the heat to low and simmer gently until the pears are very tender, 15 to 20 minutes.

Using the back of a wooden spoon or a potato masher, mash the pears until only slightly chunky. You can also transfer to a blender or food processor and pulse for a few seconds. Let cool slightly if serving right away; if packing in a bento, cool completely.

To serve, divide the cottage cheese among four small bowls or bento compartments and then press your favorite cookie cutter gently into the cottage cheese, spooning roughly 2 tablespoons of the pear sauce into the cutter. Carefully remove the cutter and finish packing the bento. You can also simply swirl in the pear sauce, no cutter required. Note that you will have leftover pear sauce.

When storing in the fridge, keep the pear sauce and the cottage cheese separate until serving.

INGREDIENT TIP: If you have additional pears on hand, core and chop one into small chunks, but do not peel. Add a sprinkling of the fresh pear to the cottage cheese and mix before topping with the pear sauce. Feel free to enjoy the rest of the fresh pear yourself.

BONUS RECIPE: For a fun breakfast, brunch, or school lunch, use the sauce in a yogurt parfait. Fill a tall glass or bento container with 2 tablespoons plain or vanilla yogurt, 1 tablespoon ginger-pear sauce, 2 tablespoons granola, and 4 raspberries, and then repeat the layers until the glass is full. The raspberries should be the top layer.

Almond, Apricot + Cranberry Granola

Cooking spray

3 cups old-fashioned oats

2 cups sliced or slivered almonds

¼ cup flaxseed

⅓ cup pure maple syrup

¼ cup extra-virgin olive oil or melted coconut oil

¼ cup brown sugar

1 teaspoon ground cinnamon

½ teaspoon sea salt

1 cup chopped dried apricots

1 cup dried cranberries

**MAKES
6 CUPS**

STORAGE
2 months
in airtight
container

PREP TIME
10 minutes
COOK TIME
45 minutes

vegan

dairy
free

gluten
free

Preheat the oven to 300°F. Coat a baking sheet with cooking spray.

In a large bowl, combine the oats, almonds, flaxseed, maple syrup, olive oil, brown sugar, cinnamon, and sea salt. Mix everything with your hands or a large spoon until well coated and combined. Pour the oat mixture onto the baking sheet and spread it out in an even layer.

Bake for 45 minutes, stirring every 15 minutes and rotating the baking sheet.

Let the granola cool on the baking sheet, then add the apricots and cranberries and mix until combined.

SUBSTITUTION TIP: To make this granola nut-free, use 2 cups sesame seeds, sunflower seeds, pepitas, or coconut flakes instead of the almonds.

BENTO
30

This is how most of our summer weeknights go: In the kitchen I toss together a couscous salad between sips of a white wine spritzer, while outside my hubby grills the chicken and the girls completely destroy our backyard. If there is even a small patch of dirt in the backyard, they will somehow get it wet and roll around in it until they are completely covered, then come to the table acting as if nothing is out of the ordinary. It's a good thing that, after dinner, both the patio table and the girls can be hosed down. But there's no dirt involved when I pack their bentos with couscous salad, carrot applesauce, and chocolate crispy treats, plus a healthy kick of edamame, kiwi fruit, and fresh blackberries.

Chicken Couscous Salad with Corn + Golden Raisins

1 (5- to 6-ounce) package couscous (about 1 cup)

2 cups cubed cooked chicken

3 ears of corn, kernels cut off, or 1 cup frozen corn, thawed

3 scallions, finely sliced

½ cup slivered almonds, toasted

⅓ cup golden raisins, roughly chopped

2 tablespoons extra-virgin olive oil

2 tablespoons apple cider or champagne vinegar

2 teaspoons honey

Salt

Freshly ground black pepper

SERVES 6

STORAGE
5 days in refrigerator

PREP TIME
20 minutes
COOK TIME
5 minutes

dairy free

Cook the couscous according to the package directions and let cool.

In a large bowl, toss together the couscous, chicken, corn, scallions, toasted almonds, and raisins.

In a small bowl, whisk together the olive oil, vinegar, honey, salt, and pepper. Drizzle the dressing over the couscous mixture and toss until everything is coated.

Serve warm or cold. If packing in a bento, it should be cold, and include an ice pack.

INGREDIENT TIP: For younger kiddos, Israeli couscous works great in this recipe and is a little easier to pick up, whether with their spoon or fingers.

Carrot Applesauce

6 apples, peeled, cored, and chopped

4 carrots, chopped

1 teaspoon ground cinnamon

½ teaspoon ground cloves

1 teaspoon pure vanilla extract

1 cup water

In a large stockpot, combine all the ingredients and bring to a boil over medium-high heat. Reduce the heat to a simmer, cover the pot, and cook, stirring occasionally, until the carrots are tender, 35 to 45 minutes. Let cool slightly.

Transfer to a blender or a food processor and pulse until it reaches your desired consistency. For a chunky applesauce, pulse for 20 seconds. For a smooth applesauce, purée on high speed for 60 to 90 seconds.

Serve warm or cold. If packing in a bento, it should be chilled first.

PREP TIP: Even though they are marketed for baby food, reusable silicone purée pouches are great to have on hand for older kids as well. Ellie, my 4-year-old, loves having a pouch between school and her afternoon activities. For an easy recipe that is full of protein and nutrients, simply fill a pouch halfway with carrot applesauce and the rest of the way with plain Greek yogurt. Seal and knead for a couple of seconds to mix the ingredients.

Brown Rice Crispy Treats with Chocolate Drizzle

FOR THE BROWN RICE CRISPY TREATS

¼ cup peanut butter, almond butter, or seed butter

½ cup honey or agave nectar

1 tablespoon coconut oil

1 teaspoon pure vanilla extract

4 cups crispy brown rice cereal

FOR THE CHOCOLATE TOPPING

¼ cup dark chocolate chips

1 teaspoon coconut oil

**MAKES
16 SQUARES**

STORAGE
1 week in
refrigerator

PREP TIME
15 minutes
COOK TIME
5 minutes
CHILL TIME
1 hour

veg

gluten
free

Line an 8-inch square baking pan with parchment paper or plastic wrap and set aside.

In a small saucepan, combine the peanut butter, honey, coconut oil, and vanilla extract and bring to a soft boil over medium heat, stirring until fully combined and smooth. Remove the pan from the heat.

Transfer the peanut butter mixture to a large bowl. Add the cereal and stir until everything is combined. Let cool until just barely warm. Pour the cereal into the baking pan and press down firmly with your hand or a spatula until it is tightly and evenly packed.

To make the chocolate topping, combine the dark chocolate chips and coconut oil in a small saucepan. Set the heat to low and stir frequently until smooth. Drizzle on top of the rice crispy treats.

Refrigerate the rice crispy treats for at least 1 hour before cutting into 16 squares.

SUBSTITUTION TIP: For toasted coconut–brown rice crispy treats, add in ½ cup toasted shredded coconut flakes with the rice cereal. With the chocolate drizzled topping, we should just call these what they are—Almond Joy Brown Rice Crispy Treats!

Summer is all about taking it easy. Given that penchant to sit around and do nothing, the recipes in this box may seem fancy, but they each take 15 minutes or less to make. My approach is to make them throughout the week for dinners, and then arrange it all in Friday's bento lunch. The chicken salad pita is made with leftover grilled chicken, the caprese salad I set aside while making a more classic bruschetta, and the wonton dippers are made for a special dessert (see the bonus recipe, page 155, for sundaes). A fresh blueberry and blackberry fruit salad and colorful cut peppers round out the bento box.

Citrus-Basil Chicken Salad in Pita

¼ cup Basil + Lemon Pesto (page 162) or store-bought pesto

2 tablespoons mayonnaise

Juice of ½ lemon

½ teaspoon grated lemon zest

Salt

Freshly ground black pepper

2 cups cubed or shredded cooked chicken

1 cup mini mozzarella balls or 1 large mozzarella ball, chopped

6 small or 4 large pita pockets

MAKES
6 SMALL OR
4 LARGE PITA
SANDWICHES

STORAGE
5 days in
refrigerator

PREP TIME
15 minutes

nut
free

In a medium bowl, whisk together the pesto, mayonnaise, lemon juice, lemon zest, salt, and pepper. Add the chicken and mozzarella and toss until everything is evenly coated.

Cut each pita pocket in half and fill with 2 to 3 heaping spoonfuls of the chicken salad. Depending on your child's age or appetite, place 2 or 3 pita halves in the bento.

INGREDIENT TIP: For a more grown-up pita pocket, add mixed green lettuce, cut tomatoes, or shredded carrots.

"Go Fish" Caprese Salad

veg / nut free / gluten free

SERVES 4

STORAGE
2 days in
refrigerator

PREP TIME
5 minutes

½ cup halved cherry tomatoes

½ cup mini mozzarella balls or 1 large
mozzarella ball, chopped

¼ cup sliced black olives

1 tablespoon thinly sliced fresh
basil leaves

1 teaspoon extra-virgin olive oil

½ teaspoon balsamic vinegar

Salt

Freshly ground black pepper

In a medium bowl, toss together the tomatoes, mozzarella balls, olives, and basil.
Drizzle on the olive oil and balsamic vinegar, then season with salt and pepper.
Gently mix with a spoon.

Serve with a thick wooden skewer or large toothpick so that your children have to
"go fish" to eat the salad. Or skip the stick and leave the job to their little fingers.

Peach + Nutmeg Yogurt Dip

veg / nut free / gluten free

MAKES 1 CUP

STORAGE
1 week in
refrigerator

PREP TIME
5 minutes
COOK TIME
15 minutes

1 cup sliced peaches, fresh or frozen

¼ cup water

2 tablespoons honey

Juice of ½ lemon

⅛ teaspoon ground nutmeg

1 cup plain Greek yogurt, 2% or full-fat

In a small saucepan, bring the peaches, water, honey, lemon juice, and nutmeg to
a boil over medium heat. Reduce the heat to a simmer and cook until there is no
more liquid in the pan, about 15 minutes. Let cool slightly.

Transfer the peaches to a blender or food processor and gently pulse until they are
still slightly chunky, about 15 seconds. In a medium bowl, spoon in the yogurt and
peaches, and gently mix them together until well combined. Let cool completely
before serving or adding to a bento box.

SUBSTITUTION TIP: If you can't find good peaches in season, use what you can
get your hands on. Nectarines or plums work well in this recipe, too.

Cinnamon + Sugar Wonton Dippers

25 wonton wrappers

3 tablespoons sugar

1 teaspoon ground cinnamon

Cooking spray

Preheat the oven to 400°F. Line two baking sheets with parchment paper or silicone mats.

On a cutting board, cut the wonton wrappers into strips or triangles, or use your favorite cookie cutter to make fun shapes.

In a small bowl, mix the sugar and cinnamon.

Lay out the cut wrappers in a single layer on the baking sheets and spray them with cooking spray, then sprinkle with the cinnamon sugar.

Bake for 5 to 7 minutes, watching closely after 5 minutes, as they tend to burn quickly. Let cool completely before adding to the bento.

BONUS RECIPE: For an extra-special dessert, these wontons make an amazingly crunchy addition to ice cream sundaes. This recipe makes 4 sundaes.

Make the wonton dippers as instructed above, let cool, and then crush 1 cup of strips into dime-size pieces.

Make the peaches as directed in step 1 of Peach + Nutmeg Yogurt Dip (page 154). When they are done cooking, smash them with the back of a spoon in the sauce-pan or chop them on a cutting board with a knife.

To make each sundae, scoop a heaping serving of your favorite vanilla bean ice cream into four serving bowls. Top the ice cream with the peaches and then sprinkle with the wonton pieces. Serve on your front porch and enjoy.

**MAKES
25 WONTONS
(ABOUT
12 SERVINGS)**

STORAGE
1 week in
airtight
container

PREP TIME
5 minutes
COOK TIME
5 minutes

vegan

nut
free

dairy
free

When all else fails, this simple cheese and bean quesadilla will be there for you—I make this for the girls all the time for a quick lunch or dinner. To keep it simple, this recipe calls for only three ingredients: tortillas, cheese, and beans. But feel free to add anything else in your fridge that you have time for—chopped cooked chicken or beef, chopped red or green bell peppers, finely chopped jalapeños, shredded spinach, or any roasted vegetable your kid enjoys. Serve with a big side of Easy-Peasy Guacamole (page 161) and some cut watermelon shapes for a fun but quick summer lunch.

Cheese + Black Bean Quesadilla

⅓ cup shredded Cheddar cheese

2 large tortillas

2 tablespoons canned black beans, rinsed and drained

Cooking spray

SERVES
1 ADULT OR
2 KIDS

PREP TIME
5 minutes
COOK TIME
8 minutes

veg

nut
free

Sprinkle the cheese all over one tortilla, then top with the black beans. Place the other tortilla on top of the beans.

Heat a medium skillet over medium heat and coat it with cooking spray. Carefully move the quesadilla into the skillet and cook for 3 to 5 minutes, flip, and cook for 3 minutes more, or until golden brown on both sides.

Transfer the quesadilla to a cutting board and let it cool for about 5 minutes before cutting into wedges or slices. Serve after cutting or let cool for an additional 10 minutes before adding to a bento box.

BONUS RECIPE: For a fun twist on summer salsa, try my favorite Strawberry + Cilantro Salsa. In a medium bowl, gently stir together 2 cups hulled and chopped strawberries (or 1 pint), ⅓ cup finely chopped red onion, ½ cup finely chopped fresh cilantro, ½ minced seeded jalapeño (optional), juice of 1 lime, and 1 minced garlic clove until all ingredients are combined. Serve with your favorite chips, cheese quesadilla, fish tacos, or any black bean burritos.

6

Staples for All Seasons

These are a collection of my favorite basic recipes, the ones I know off the top of my head and use at least once a week, especially the pizza crust, which I make all the time! These recipes are meant to be on the basic side, leaving you plenty of room to customize the recipe with additional spices, herbs, or other flavors to make it your own and suit what you are serving it with. While simple in nature, these recipes still deliver big in the taste department. Easy to make, easy to customize, easy to eat!

Whole-Wheat Pizza Dough

MAKES 1 LARGE PIZZA

STORAGE (after rising): 4 days in refrigerator or 2 months in freezer

PREP TIME: 25 minutes

RISING TIME: 30 minutes to 12 hours

1 cup warm water

1 packet active dry yeast

1 teaspoon honey

2 cups white whole-wheat flour

2 tablespoons extra-virgin olive oil, plus additional for oiling the bowl

1 teaspoon salt

In a large bowl or the bowl of a stand mixer, mix the water, yeast, and honey. Let sit for 5 minutes or until it becomes bubbly.

Add the flour, olive oil, and salt and mix until well incorporated. If using a stand mixer, use the dough hook and let the machine knead the dough for 3 minutes. The dough should be smooth and not sticky to the touch. If sticky, add in more flour, 1 tablespoon at a time. If dry and not holding together in a ball, add in more water, 1 tablespoon at a time. If mixing by hand, sprinkle a little flour onto the counter and knead by hand for 2 to 3 minutes.

Lightly oil the mixing bowl, place the dough ball in the bowl, and lightly oil the top of the dough. Cover the bowl with a clean, dry kitchen towel and let the dough rise for at least 30 minutes or up to 12 hours. I usually make my dough in the morning before school drop-off and it's ready at dinnertime.

Place the risen dough on a lightly floured counter and knead it a few times. Wait 15 minutes and then shape or roll into a pizza shape.

INGREDIENT TIP: This dough is super forgiving and you can use all-purpose, white whole-wheat, whole-wheat, or gluten-free flour. I often make a 50/50 mixture of whole-wheat and white whole-wheat for our family pizza night. Play around with flour combinations to find out what is your family's favorite.

Easy-Peasy Guacamole

vegan / nut free / dairy free / gluten free

SERVES 2

STORAGE: 1 day in refrigerator

PREP TIME: 5 minutes

1 ripe avocado, pitted and peeled

Juice of 1 lime

1 garlic clove, minced, or ¼ teaspoon garlic powder

1 tablespoon finely diced red onion or ⅛ teaspoon onion powder

OPTIONAL MIX-INS
(choose 1 or 2)

¼ cup chopped tomatoes

1 tablespoon finely chopped fresh cilantro

¼ jalapeño pepper, seeded and finely chopped

¼ cup mango chunks

¼ cup pineapple chunks

In a medium bowl, smash the avocado with the back of a fork. Add the lime juice, garlic, and onion and mix well. Mix in whichever of the suggested toppings appeal to you.

BENTO PACKING TIP: Small metal containers with lids work great for keeping the guacamole fresh in a bento. If storing in the fridge, press a layer of plastic wrap as close as possible over the top of the guacamole, trying to not let any air in—that's what turns the avocado brown.

Homemade Croutons

vegan / nut free / dairy free

MAKES 4 CUPS

STORAGE: 1 week in airtight container

PREP TIME: 25 minutes

COOK TIME: 20 minutes

3 tablespoons extra-virgin olive oil

8 slices bread of your choosing, cubed

1 teaspoon garlic powder

1 teaspoon salt

Place a large skillet over medium heat and add the olive oil. Toss in the bread cubes and stir until evenly coated with the oil. Sprinkle the garlic powder and salt over the bread and cook until slightly golden, 3 to 5 minutes. Reduce the heat to low and cook, stirring occasionally, until brown and slightly crispy, 10 to 12 minutes more. Transfer the croutons to a plate and let cool completely. They will continue to harden as they cool.

Basil + Lemon Pesto

veg / nut free / gluten free

MAKES 1 CUP

STORAGE: 1 week in refrigerator, 1 month in freezer

PREP TIME: 5 minutes

2 cups fresh basil leaves

Juice of ½ lemon

2 garlic cloves, peeled

½ cup grated
Parmesan cheese

Salt

Freshly ground
black pepper

½ cup extra-virgin
olive oil

Combine the basil, lemon juice, garlic, Parmesan, salt, and pepper in a food processor or blender. Pulse a few times to get the ingredients chopped and mixed.

With the machine running at high speed, slowly drizzle in the olive oil. Continue blending until the ingredients are well incorporated, about 30 seconds.

Healthy Ranch Dip or Dressing

veg / nut free / gluten free

MAKES ¾ CUP

STORAGE: 2 weeks in refrigerator

PREP TIME: 5 minutes

½ cup plain Greek
yogurt, 2% or full-fat

¼ cup mayonnaise

¼ cup milk (optional)

Juice of ½ lemon

½ teaspoon dried dill

½ teaspoon
dried parsley

¼ teaspoon
garlic powder

¼ teaspoon
onion powder

In a medium bowl, combine all ingredients and whisk until creamy and smooth. The milk will make this more of a dressing consistency. For more of a dip, omit the milk.

Basic Vinaigrette

veg / nut free / dairy free / gluten free

MAKES ¾ CUP

STORAGE: 2 weeks in refrigerator

PREP TIME: 5 minutes

3 tablespoons
balsamic vinegar

1 teaspoon
Dijon mustard

1 teaspoon honey

Salt

Freshly ground
black pepper

½ cup extra-virgin
olive oil

In a small bowl, whisk together the vinegar, mustard, honey, salt, and pepper. Then slowly whisk in the olive oil until it thickens and emulsifies.

The vinaigrette will become hard when chilled so make sure to bring it to room temperature before use. Stir and serve.

PREP TIP: If you're in a rush, pour all of the ingredients into a mason jar, screw on the lid, and shake it for 1 minute. The best part is that you can store the extra dressing right in the jar!

INGREDIENT TIP: For vinaigrette with a kick, add 1 garlic clove, minced, or 1 tablespoon of herbs such as chives, parsley, dill, thyme, or oregano.

Simple Lemon + Cumin Hummus

vegan / nut free / gluten free

MAKES 2 CUPS

STORAGE: 1 week in refrigerator

PREP TIME: 5 minutes

1 (15-ounce) can
chickpeas, reserve ½
cup liquid

Juice of 1 lemon

1 clove garlic, minced

½ teaspoon
ground cumin

½ teaspoon salt

1 tablespoon tahini or
½ teaspoon toasted
sesame oil

2 tablespoons extra-
virgin olive oil

In a food processor or blender, add the chickpeas with reserved liquid, lemon juice, garlic, cumin, salt, and tahini or toasted sesame oil, and pulse until all the ingredients are combined. With the machine running, drizzle in the olive oil and blend for 60 seconds, scraping down the sides.

INGREDIENT TIP: Have fun with this basic recipe by adding ingredient combinations.

For roasted red pepper hummus, add to the food processor 4 ounces jarred roasted red peppers (drained), and a pinch of cayenne pepper, with the chickpeas.

For pesto hummus, add to the food processor ¼ cup Basil + Lemon Pesto (page 162) or your favorite store-bought brand of pesto, along with the chickpeas.

For beet hummus, add to the food processor 1 small cooked beet and ¼ teaspoon ground coriander, along with the chickpeas.

THE DIRTY DOZEN
& THE CLEAN FIFTEEN

A nonprofit and environmental watch-dog organization called Environmental Working Group (EWG) looks at data supplied by the U.S. Department of Agriculture (USDA) and the Food and Drug Administration (FDA) about pesticide residues and compiles a list each year of the best and worst pesticide loads found in commercial crops. You can use these lists to decide which fruits and vegetables to buy organic to minimize your exposure to pesticides and which produce is considered safe enough to skip the organics. This does not mean they are pesticide-free, though, so wash these fruits and vegetables thoroughly.

These lists change every year, so make sure you look up the most recent before you fill your shopping cart. You'll find the most recent lists as well as a guide to pesticides in produce at http://EWG.org/FoodNews.

The Dirty Dozen

- Apples
- Celery
- Cherries
- Cherry tomatoes
- Cucumbers
- Grapes
- Nectarines
- Peaches
- Spinach
- Strawberries
- Sweet bell peppers
- Tomatoes

Plus produce contaminated with highly toxic organophosphate insecticides:

- Hot peppers
- Kale/collard greens

The Clean Fifteen

- Asparagus
- Avocados
- Cabbage
- Cantaloupe
- Cauliflower
- Eggplant
- Grapefruit
- Honeydew melon
- Kiwi
- Mangos
- Onions
- Papayas
- Pineapples
- Sweet corn
- Sweet peas (frozen)

MEASUREMENT CONVERSIONS

VOLUME EQUIVALENTS (LIQUID)

US STANDARD	US STANDARD (OUNCES)	METRIC (APPROXIMATE)
2 tablespoons	1 fl. oz.	30 mL
¼ cup	2 fl. oz.	60 mL
½ cup	4 fl. oz.	120 mL
1 cup	8 fl. oz.	240 mL
1½ cups	12 fl. oz.	355 mL
2 cups or 1 pint	16 fl. oz.	475 mL
4 cups or 1 quart	32 fl. oz.	1 L
1 gallon	128 fl. oz.	4 L

OVEN TEMPERATURES

FAHRENHEIT (F)	CELSIUS (C) (APPROXIMATE)
250°	120°
300°	150°
325°	165°
350°	180°
375°	190°
400°	200°
425°	220°
450°	230°

VOLUME EQUIVALENTS (DRY)

US STANDARD	METRIC (APPROXIMATE)
⅛ teaspoon	0.5 mL
¼ teaspoon	1 mL
½ teaspoon	2 mL
¾ teaspoon	4 mL
1 teaspoon	5 mL
1 tablespoon	15 mL
¼ cup	59 mL
⅓ cup	79 mL
½ cup	118 mL
⅔ cup	156 mL
¾ cup	177 mL
1 cup	235 mL
2 cups or 1 pint	475 mL
3 cups	700 mL
4 cups or 1 quart	1 L
½ gallon	2 L
1 gallon	4 L

WEIGHT EQUIVALENTS

US STANDARD	METRIC (APPROXIMATE)
½ ounce	15 g
1 ounce	30 g
2 ounces	60 g
4 ounces	115 g
8 ounces	225 g
12 ounces	340 g
16 ounces or 1 pound	455 g

RESOURCES

In photographing the bento boxes for this book, I used 10 different boxes that range from two separate compartments to six. Most can easily be found and purchased online, although one came from a local Japanese market. Here are the boxes I used:

PlanetBox Rover
www.planetbox.com

ECOlunchbox Three-in-One Bento
www.planetbox.com

Smart Bento Box
www.smartbentobox.com

ECOlunchbox Kid's Tray
www.planetbox.com

thinksport GO2 Container
gothinkbaby.com

thinksport GO4th Insulated Container
gothinkbaby.com

Innobaby Din Din Smart Bus Platter
innobaby.com

Steeltainer 5 Compartment Divided Lunch Container
www.steeltainer.com

Steeltainer Compact Divided Snack Container
www.steeltainer.com

Manufacturer unknown
Purchased at Tokyo Fish Market, Berkeley, CA

RECIPE INDEX BY BENTO BOX

BENTO 1

BENTO 2

BENTO 3

BENTO 4

BENTO 5

BENTO 6

BENTO 7
Spinach Pesto Pizza Rollups, 57
Simple Pizza Sauce, 58
Alternative Main: Veggie-Loaded
    Pepperoni Pizza Rollups, 59

QUICK BENTO 8
Grilled Cheese + Apple
    Sandwich, 61

BENTO 9
5-Layer Bean Dip, 65
Baked Spiced Tortilla Dippers, 66
White Chocolate + Pistachio
    Pretzels, 67

BENTO 10
Coconut Rice with Snap Peas +
    Edamame, 69
Dark Chocolate Haystacks, 70
Alternative Main: Easy Veggie +
    Pineapple Rice, 71

BENTO 11
Kid-Friendly Veggie Chili, 73
Broccoli + Cheddar Corn Muffins, 74
Cocoa + Cinnamon Spiced Nuts, 75

BENTO 12
Seed Butter + Jelly Sandwich
    on a Stick, 77
Sweet Cajun Party Mix, 78
Whole-Wheat Chocolate Chip
    Cookies, 79

BENTO 13
Italian Turkey Meatballs, 81
Super Cinnamon Crackers, 82
Alternative Main: Vietnamese
    Meatballs, 83

BENTO 14
DIY Garlic Noodles with Chicken,
    Bacon, Peas + Cheese, 85
Raspberry + Orange Oat Bars, 86
Alternative Main: Sun-Dried
    Tomato Pesto Pasta Salad with
    Chicken, Olives + Feta, 87

BENTO 15
Pesto, Corn + Zucchini Pizza, 89
Sweet Peppers + Cheese Pizza, 90
Chicken + Ranch Pita Pizza with
    Spinach + Tomatoes, 91

QUICK BENTO 16
Pesto + Turkey Tortilla Rollup, 93

BENTO 17
Tuna Slaw + Cucumber + Olive
   Sandwiches on a Stick, 97
Herbed Parmesan Popcorn, 98
Alternative Main: Curried Chickpea
   Salad, 99

BENTO 18
Carrot + Beet Cream Cheese
   Sandwiches, 101
Baked Sweet Potato Chips, 102
Seed Butter Cookies, 103

BENTO 19
Apple + Cranberry Chicken
   Salad, 105
Raspberry + Lemon Fruit
   Leather, 106
Alternative Main: Southwest
   Chicken Salad, 107

BENTO 20
Tofu Bahn Mi on a Stick, 109
Cilantro Dipping Sauce, 110
Crunchy Moroccan-Spiced
   Chickpeas, 111

BENTO 21
Crispy Chicken Strips, 113
Honey-Mustard Dipping Sauce, 114
Easy Pan-Roasted Asparagus +
   Rosemary, 115

BENTO 22
Spring Veggie + Mint Pesto Pasta
   Salad, 117
Olive Oil + Walnut Brownies, 118
Honey-Mustard Spiced Pretzels, 119

BENTO 23
Easy Whole-Wheat Pretzel
   Bites, 121
Blackberry-Mustard Dipping
   Sauce, 122
Alternative Main: Easy Baked
   Falafel, 123

QUICK BENTO 24
Curried Egg Salad, 125
Fancy Ants on a Log, 125

BENTO 25
Deconstructed Cobb Salad, 129
Creamy Feta Dipping Sauce, 130
Alternative Main: Deconstructed
Chicken Waldorf Salad, 131

BENTO 26
Mais Pizza, 133
Chocolate Avocado Pudding, 135
ABC Salad with Lemon
Dressing, 134

BENTO 27
Sweet Turkey Sandwich
on a Stick, 137
Cinnamon Apple Chips, 138
No-Cook Chocolate Chip
Energy Balls, 139

BENTO 28
Sesame Soba Noodle Salad, 141
Watermelon + Strawberries with
Feta + Mint, 142
Alternative Main: Crunchy Asian
Chopped Salad, 143

BENTO 29
Super Green Spinach Muffins, 145
Ginger–Pear Sauce over Cottage
Cheese, 146
Almond, Apricot + Cranberry
Granola, 147

BENTO 30
Chicken Couscous Salad with
Corn + Golden Raisins, 149
Carrot Applesauce, 150
Brown Rice Crispy Treats with
Chocolate Drizzle, 151

BENTO 31
Citrus-Basil Chicken Salad in
Pita, 153
"Go Fish" Caprese Salad, 154
Peach + Nutmeg Yogurt Dip, 154
Cinnamon + Sugar Wonton
Dippers, 155

QUICK BENTO 32
Cheese + Black Bean Quesadilla, 157

RECIPE INDEX BY DIETARY LABEL

ACKNOWLEDGMENTS

First and foremost, I want to thank my amazing editor Stacy Wagner-Kinnear. I am so glad that we got to partner together on another book and that we both survived the process, if only by a thread! I still don't know how I managed to do so much in such little time, but your humor and love for my vision makes the entire process addicting and, dare I say it, fun. It's time for you to exit my brain, for now.

Katy Brown, if only there were enough words. My heart will always be intertwined with yours for what we went through while making this book. Yet, somehow, we pulled ourselves together (with lots of virtual hugs) and made something beautiful. Your guidance and expertise were critical in creating this amazing finished product.

Thank you also to Frances Baca, Caroline Lee, and the rest of the Callisto team that made this book.

Holly Smith, your energy for marketing my books is contagious and I apologize in advance for my long overdue emails to you.

Thank you to Ms. Casey for being the best teacher a mom could ever ask for and also for letting me bring my test recipes into Ellie's class.

To Mary, for always being my foodie friend. To Lindsey, who shares my twisted sense of humor. To Rachel, who is always there for me. You ladies make my days sane by always keeping my cup (of wine) full.

In memory of my big brother Ryan, I will love you forever and always.

To my mom and dad, for always believing in my ideas—Every.Single.Crazy.One. You are the best parents and grandparents a girl could ask for.

Of course, thank you to my little ladies, Elliette and Parker. You will always be the driving force behind my books and blog. I love you more than you will ever know.

To my hubby, Andy, thank you for always and forever being there for me, and for eating lunch-for-dinner every single night for the last couple of months. I couldn't have done this without your support and love, you better believe it.

And finally, thank you to my readers and followers, both longtime and new. This book would not be here if it weren't for you. You push me to keep going, to get up an extra 5 minutes earlier in the morning to take a pretty shot of Ellie's lunches (even though I may be slightly cursing you when the alarm goes off), and to keep cooking up delicious meals for both my family and yours. What makes this all worthwhile is getting to know so many of my readers, so please comment on my posts or email me directly with your feedback, thoughts, or just to say hi.